ABC

delicious.

Simply the best

delicious.

Simply the best

celebrating 10 delicious years

valli little

Welcome

It's hard to believe that it's been 10 years since a small group of us got together to plan the first issue of *delicious.* magazine. At that initial meeting, we hoped for, but never dreamed of, the success that was to unfold.

During the past decade, we've been fortunate enough to have met and worked with fantastic chefs, as well as truly talented home cooks. We've travelled this country and around the world visiting great culinary destinations and eating many incredible dishes along the way. It has been an amazing journey and certainly one worth celebrating.

Simply the Best – our seventh cookbook – pays homage to this milestone birthday. The 120 new recipes in these pages are a nod to our past, reflecting the wonderful places, people and food that have inspired us. Each dish also demonstrates what we do best at *delicious.* – create exciting and accessible recipes for dedicated foodies of all ages.

So let's raise a celebratory glass of Champagne to say, 'Happy 10th birthday *delicious.* magazine. May there be many more years of happy cooking ahead.'

Valli

Contents

8 ALMOST FRENCH
Take a cue from iconic Parisian bistros
and re-create classic dishes with a twist.

32 POP-UP DINNER
Get on board with the latest food trend and
host an impromptu dinner party at home.

56 LIFE'S A BEACH
Make the most of a summer's day
with food that's simple and refreshing.

80 A MOVEABLE FEAST
Some dishes are best savoured alfresco
on a rug laid out in the dappled shade.

104 KEEPING UP APPEARANCES
Add a few clever flourishes to the plate
and you'll be sure to wow your guests.

128 EAST MEETS WEST
From fishcakes to salt-and-pepper quail, try
food inspired by the exotic flavours of Asia.

152 BEYOND WICKED
Stunning desserts that are more than
a little bit naughty, but oh-so nice.

176 TRATTORIA AT HOME
Be it pizza, pasta or tiramisu, rustic
trattoria-style dishes offer the best of Italy.

200 DATE NIGHT
You don't need a special occasion to light
some candles and enjoy a dinner for two.

224 GET COSY
Recipes that warm the kitchen and the heart
– indulge with the ultimate comfort food.

248 PLAYING WITH FIRE
Sparks will fly when you head outdoors
to cook these recipes on the barbecue.

272 COOL YULE
So this is Christmas. Here's our take
on the festive feast, minus the fuss.

296 BASIC RECIPES
298 INDEX

Almost French

For as long as I can remember, I've had a passion for all things French. On my travels, I've been lucky enough to eat in some of France's finest restaurants, as well as local bistros that serve simple fare. The depth of this cuisine always inspires me. In this chapter, I've taken some of my favourite ingredients – such as croissants, crepes and goat's cheese – and given them my own twist. That's why it's called 'Almost French'.

Apple & goat's cheese salad

1 Granny Smith apple
1 Pink Lady apple
Juice of 1 lemon
½ red onion
1 baby fennel
150g aged goat's cheese*
2 tbs extra virgin olive oil
½ tsp wholegrain mustard
2 tsp Dijon mustard
1 tsp truffle honey*,
  plus extra to drizzle
1 cup micro salad leaves*

Core and thinly slice the apples into rounds (a mandoline is ideal). Toss the apple slices with most of the lemon juice, reserving 2 teaspoons for the dressing, and set aside.

Slice the onion and fennel very thinly (a mandoline is ideal) and cut the cheese into 5mm slices. Set aside.

Whisk the oil, mustards, truffle honey and reserved 2 teaspoons lemon juice together until combined, then season and set aside.

Toss the salad leaves with a little of the dressing. Stack the apple slices, onion, fennel, goat's cheese and salad leaves in layers on serving plates. Drizzle with the remaining dressing and extra truffle honey and serve. **Serves 4**

* Aged goat's cheese (substitute regular firm goat's cheese) and truffle honey are available from selected delis. Micro salad leaves are available from farmers' markets and selected greengrocers.

Twice-baked soufflé

These soufflés have been a permanent fixture on my dinner-party standby list for years. They never fail to impress and you can even prepare them a day in advance: just pop them in the oven for a few minutes and they will miraculously rise again.

50g unsalted butter
½ cup (75g) plain flour
2 cups (500ml) milk
Pinch of grated nutmeg
4 eggs, separated,
   plus 1 extra eggwhite
150g baby spinach leaves,
   blanched, squeezed dry
120g soft goat's cheese,
   crumbled
½ cup (40g) finely grated
   parmesan cheese
½ cup (125ml) pure
   (thin) cream
⅓ cup (35g) toasted walnuts
Micro salad leaves*, to serve

Preheat the oven to 180°C and grease six 1-cup (250ml) dariole moulds or ovenproof teacups.

Melt the butter in a saucepan over low heat and add the flour. Cook, stirring, for 1 minute. Whisk in the milk, nutmeg and some salt and pepper. Bring to just below boiling point, then whisk for 2 minutes or until very thick and smooth. Add the egg yolks, one at a time, beating well after each addition. Stir in the blanched spinach, goat's cheese and half the parmesan.

In a clean, dry bowl, whisk the 5 eggwhites with a pinch of salt until soft peaks form. Fold one-third of the eggwhite into the cheese mixture to loosen, then fold in the remaining eggwhite until just combined.

Place the moulds in a baking dish and divide the soufflé mixture among them. Run your finger around the inside edge of the mould (this will ensure the soufflés will rise evenly), then pour in enough boiling water to come halfway up the sides of the moulds. Bake in the oven for 15-20 minutes until puffed and golden. Remove from the baking dish, cool, then invert onto a greased baking tray. The soufflés can be chilled at this stage for up to 24 hours, if desired.

When almost ready to serve, preheat the oven to 180°C.

Pour cream over the soufflés and sprinkle with remaining ¼ cup (20g) parmesan. Bake soufflés for 10-12 minutes until puffed and golden. Scatter with walnuts and salad leaves and serve immediately. **Makes 6**

* Micro salad leaves are available from farmers' markets and selected greengrocers.

Yesterday's croissants

Croissants always look so tempting sitting in the bakery window and I usually end up buying too many. This is the perfect way to turn leftover croissants into a savoury brunch or simple supper.

6 day-old croissants
25g unsalted butter
25g plain flour
200ml milk
1 tbs wholegrain mustard
Finely grated zest of 1 lemon
100g gruyere cheese,
    finely grated
6 slices Black Forest ham*

Preheat the oven to 180°C and the grill to high.

Split the croissants lengthways and toast under the grill, cut-side up, for 2-3 minutes until golden.

Melt the butter in a saucepan over medium-low heat. Add the flour and cook, stirring, for 1 minute. Add the milk, reduce heat to low and whisk for 5-6 minutes until thick and smooth. Add the mustard, lemon zest and three-quarters of the cheese, then season well.

Lay the ham slices on the croissant bases and spread with most of the cheese sauce. Sandwich with the croissant tops and spread each top with a little of the remaining sauce. Sprinkle with the remaining 25g cheese and bake for 6 minutes or until bubbling and golden. **Serves 6**

* Black Forest ham is from selected delis; substitute smoked ham.

Bouillabaisse in a bag

Here is a quirky way to cook bouillabaisse:
in paper or *en papillote*, as they say in France.

12 green prawns, peeled
(tails intact), deveined

350g skinless boneless
white fish (such as ling)

350g skinless salmon fillet,
pin-boned

12 scallops, roe removed

12 vine-ripened cherry
tomatoes, halved

1 cup (150g) podded broad
beans, blanched, peeled

1 cup (120g) frozen
baby peas

1 cup dill sprigs

1 lemon, thinly sliced

½ cup (125ml) dry white wine

Extra virgin olive oil,
to drizzle

1 tbs roughly chopped
flat-leaf parsley

Aioli (see 'Basics', p 296) and
boiled potatoes (optional),
to serve

Preheat oven to 180°C.

To prepare the parcels, cut twelve 1m sheets of baking paper. Place 1 sheet on a work surface, then lay another sheet on top at an angle to form an X-shape. Repeat with remaining baking paper to make 6 parcels.

Divide the prawns, fish, scallops, tomatoes, beans and peas among the parcels. Season well, then divide three-quarters each of the dill sprigs and lemon slices among the parcels. Drizzle with the wine and a little olive oil, then seal the parcels by gathering up the sides to the middle, scrunching the top and securing with kitchen string.

Place the parcels in the oven and bake for 10-12 minutes or until the seafood is just cooked through and the vegetables are tender.

Bring the parcels to the table and allow each guest to unwrap their own. Serve with chopped parsley, aioli, boiled potatoes and remaining dill sprigs and lemon. **Serves 6**

Duck breast with spiced orange sauce

4 oranges

4 x 200g duck breasts, skin lightly scored

1 tsp five-spice powder

⅓ firmly packed cup (80g) brown sugar

50ml red wine vinegar

1 cinnamon quill

2 star anise

½ cup (125ml) Grand Marnier*

2 cups (240g) baby green peas, blanched

Mint leaves, to serve

Zest all oranges, juice 2 oranges and set aside. Remove any peel and white pith from the remaining 2 oranges, then slice into thin rounds and set aside.

Pat the duck breasts dry with paper towel. Combine five-spice powder with 2 teaspoons sea salt, then rub onto the duck breasts.

Place a non-stick frypan over low heat and cook the duck, skin-side down, for 10 minutes or until the fat renders. Increase heat to medium and cook for 3 minutes or until skin is crispy and golden. Turn, then cook for a further 3 minutes for medium-rare. Transfer the duck to a plate and rest, loosely covered with foil, while you make the sauce.

Drain the excess fat from the pan, then return the pan to low heat. Add the sugar and vinegar to the pan, stirring to dissolve the sugar. Add cinnamon and star anise, then cook for 3-4 minutes, swirling the pan occasionally, until a golden caramel. Carefully add the Grand Marnier and orange juice and zest, then simmer for 5 minutes or until thickened. Add the orange slices and any resting juices from the duck to the pan and cook for 1-2 minutes to warm through.

Slice the duck breast and divide among serving plates. Drizzle with the warm orange sauce. Serve with baby green peas and garnish with the mint leaves and orange slices. **Serves 4**

* Grand Marnier is available from bottleshops.

Bon Appetit! It's a simple expression,
but it seems to say it all.

Onglet with Cafe de Paris butter

There's a restaurant in Paris called L'Entrecôte where they serve a dish similar to this. I pay them a visit each time I'm in the city.

2 tsp dried herbes
   de Provence *
2 tbs extra virgin olive oil
1kg onglet *, trimmed
French fries and watercress,
   to serve

Cafe de Paris butter

125g unsalted butter,
   softened
1 tsp Dijon mustard
2 tsp Worcestershire sauce
¼ cup (60ml) tomato sauce
   (ketchup)
1 tsp mild curry powder
1 tbs finely chopped eschalot
1 garlic clove,
   finely chopped
6 anchovy fillets in oil,
   drained, finely chopped
2 tbs chopped flat-leaf
   parsley
1 tbs chopped tarragon
1 tsp thyme leaves

For the Cafe de Paris butter, place all the ingredients in a bowl and mix together with a fork until well combined. Place on a sheet of foil or plastic wrap and shape the butter into a log. Roll up in the foil or plastic wrap and twist the ends to seal. Chill until firm.

Meanwhile, preheat a chargrill pan or barbecue to high heat.

Combine herbes de Provence, oil and some salt and pepper in a bowl. Brush the beef with the oil mixture, then cook for 4-6 minutes each side for rare or until cooked to your liking. Remove from the pan and set aside to rest, loosely covered with foil, for 8 minutes.

Thinly slice the beef and divide among 6 plates, then top with slices of Cafe de Paris butter. (Remaining butter will keep in the freezer for up to 2 months.) Serve with French fries and watercress. **Serves 6**

* Herbes de Provence (Provençal herbs) is a classic blend of herbs and lavender flowers traditionally used in French cuisine, available from Herbie's Spices (herbies.com.au). Onglet is a cut of beef that is also known as skirt or hanger steak.

Orange lavender syrup cake

250g unsalted butter,
   softened

1 cup (220g) caster sugar

4 eggs

⅓ cup (50g) plain flour,
   sifted

2 tsp baking powder

Finely grated zest and juice
   of 2 oranges

250g fine semolina

2 cups (250g) almond meal

120g thick Greek-style
   yoghurt

250g punnet strawberries,
   halved or quartered

Syrup

Finely grated zest and juice
   of 2 oranges

1 tbs dried lavender
   flowers*

2 cinnamon quills

1¼ cups (275g) caster sugar

Preheat the oven to 170°C. Grease a 23cm round springform pan, line the base with baking paper and lightly dust the sides with flour, shaking off any excess.

Beat the butter and sugar in an electric mixer until thick and pale. Add the eggs, one at a time, beating well after each addition. Fold in the flour and baking powder, followed by the orange zest, semolina and almond meal. Add orange juice and yoghurt and gently stir until combined. Pour into the prepared pan and bake for 1 hour or until a skewer inserted into the centre comes out clean. Cool in the pan for 5 minutes.

Meanwhile, for the syrup, place all the ingredients in a saucepan with 1½ cups (375ml) water. Stir over low heat to dissolve the sugar, then simmer for 20-25 minutes until slightly thickened.

Prick the surface of the warm cake all over with a skewer. Slowly drizzle over half the syrup, then allow to cool.

Toss the strawberries in the remaining syrup, then drizzle over the cake and serve. **Serves 6-8**

✳ Dried lavender flowers are available from selected delis and Herbie's Spices (herbies.com.au).

Coconut crepe cake

7 egg yolks
180g caster sugar
3 tsp grated lime zest
2 tbs cornflour
200ml milk
400ml coconut milk
200ml pure (thin) cream
1 cup (90g) desiccated
   coconut
Icing sugar, to dust

Crepes
1 cup (150g) plain flour
3 eggs
2 tbs caster sugar
40g unsalted butter, melted,
   cooled, plus extra melted
   butter to brush
1 cup (250ml) coconut milk
300ml milk

Passionfruit caramel
Pulp from 6-8 passionfruits
150g caster sugar

Grease and line a 20cm springform cake pan with plastic wrap, leaving plenty overhanging the sides.

Whisk together yolks, caster sugar, zest, cornflour and a pinch of salt. Place milk, coconut milk and cream in a pan over medium-high heat and bring to just below boiling point. Remove from heat and pour over egg mixture. Return mixture to a clean saucepan and cook over very low heat for 5-6 minutes, stirring, until mixture has thickened. Stir in desiccated coconut, then transfer to a bowl. Cover surface with plastic wrap and chill.

Meanwhile, for the crepes, place flour, eggs, sugar, butter, coconut milk and milk in a food processor. Whiz until smooth, then strain into a jug. Stand at room temperature for 30 minutes. Brush a 20cm crepe pan or non-stick frypan with butter and place over medium heat. Pour in just enough crepe batter to coat the base of the pan, swirling to cover. Cook for 1-2 minutes each side until lightly golden. Repeat with remaining batter, brushing the pan with more butter as needed and stacking the cooked crepes between baking paper. Cool.

Place a crepe in the prepared pan and spread with a thin layer of the coconut custard. Continue layers with remaining crepes and custard, finishing with a crepe. Fold over the overhanging wrap to cover, then press down gently. Chill for 4 hours or overnight until set.

Meanwhile, for the caramel, place the passionfruit pulp in a food processor and pulse several times to loosen the seeds from pulp. Strain into a jug, pressing down on the solids. Reserve ¼ cup seeds, then discard remaining solids. Measure ½ cup (125ml) passionfruit juice and set aside. Place caster sugar and 30ml water in a pan over low heat, stirring until sugar dissolves. Increase heat to medium and cook, without stirring, for 3-4 minutes until a golden caramel. Remove from heat and carefully stir in the passionfruit juice. Return to low heat and stir for 1-2 minutes until thickened. Cool slightly, then add passionfruit seeds and chill.

Dust cake with icing sugar and serve with caramel. **Serves 6-8**

Mille-feuille with praline cream and raspberries

2 sheets frozen puff
    pastry, thawed
½ cup (70g) icing sugar,
    sifted
½ cup (110g) caster sugar
¼ cup (40g) blanched
    almonds, toasted
1 cup (250g) mascarpone
2 x 125g punnets
    raspberries
1 small mango, sliced

Preheat the oven to 200°C. Line 2 baking trays with baking paper and lightly grease another baking tray.

Cut the pastry into 24 rectangles, each measuring 12cm x 4cm. Divide between 2 lined baking trays and dust with half the icing sugar. Lay baking paper sheets over the pastry and place heavy baking trays on top to weigh down. Bake for 25 minutes or until pastry is golden. Cool.

Meanwhile, place the caster sugar in a saucepan with 2 tablespoons water and cook over low heat, swirling the pan occasionally, until the sugar has dissolved. Increase heat to medium-high and cook for a further 3-4 minutes, swirling the pan occasionally, until a golden caramel. Remove from heat and add the almonds, then pour onto the greased baking tray. Allow to cool.

When the praline has set, break into shards, place in a food processor and whiz until coarsely ground. Reserve 1 tablespoon praline, then combine the remaining praline with the mascarpone. Set aside.

Dust half the cooked pastry rectangles with the remaining icing sugar. Carefully heat a metal skewer over an open flame until very hot, then press the skewer onto the sugar-dusted pastry in a crisscross pattern – you will need to reheat the skewer each time.

To assemble, top the undusted pastry rectangles with the mascarpone mixture, a few raspberries and a slice of mango, then carefully top with the sugar-dusted pastry rectangles. Garnish with any remaining raspberries and the reserved praline to serve. **Makes 12**

Apple tarte Tatin

I love tarte Tatin, but I often find it too sweet and cloying. The addition of pomegranate molasses seems to cut through the sweetness perfectly.

6 Granny Smith apples

1 tbs lemon juice

175g caster sugar

2 tbs pomegranate
   molasses *

375g block puff pastry

1 tsp ground cinnamon

300ml thickened cream

Preheat the oven to 180°C.

Peel, core and quarter the apples, then toss with lemon juice. Set aside.

Place the sugar in an ovenproof frypan or Tatin dish with 2 tablespoons water over low heat, stirring until the has sugar dissolved. Increase heat to medium and cook for 3-4 minutes, swirling the pan occasionally, until a golden caramel. Remove from the heat and carefully arrange the apples in a single layer over the caramel, packing in quite tightly. Drizzle the apples with the pomegranate molasses. Roll out pastry on a lightly floured work surface to 3-4mm thick, then place over the filling and tuck in the sides. Bake for 25 minutes or until puffed and golden. Remove from the oven and rest in the pan for 10 minutes.

Meanwhile, whisk cinnamon and cream together until soft peaks form.

Invert the apple tarte Tatin onto a serving plate and serve with the cinnamon cream. **Serves 6**

* Pomegranate molasses is from selected supermarkets and delis.

Pop-up dinner

Here one day, gone the next, pop-up restaurants are appearing in art galleries, parks and even private living rooms. I just love the idea – it's fun, new and there are no restrictions. So why not throw out the rule book and create a pop-up dinner at home? Here are some casual restaurant-style dishes that are easy enough to put together any night of the week.

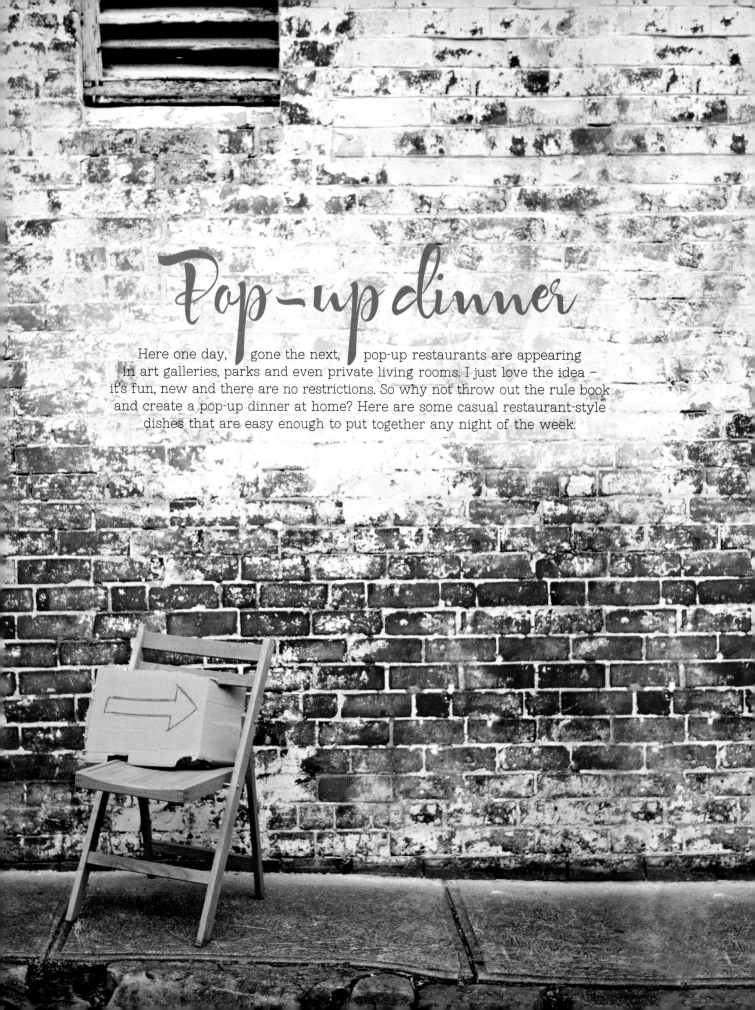

Fillet of beef with three-mustard sauce

This three-mustard sauce is so simple and is the perfect partner for beef.
It's ideal for a midweek dinner when you want to dress up your dishes.

2 tbs olive oil

1kg piece centre-cut beef
    fillet, trimmed

800g kumara, peeled,
    chopped

¼ cup (60ml) milk

20g unsalted butter

Watercress, to serve

Three-mustard sauce

1 cup (300g) whole-egg
    mayonnaise

½ cup (120g) creme fraiche

1 tbs wholegrain mustard

2 tbs Dijon mustard

1 tsp wasabi paste

1 tbs horseradish cream

Preheat the oven to 180°C.

Heat the oil in an ovenproof frypan over medium-high heat. Season the beef and cook, turning, for 3-4 minutes until browned all over. Transfer to the oven and roast for 20 minutes for medium-rare or until cooked to your liking. Transfer beef to a plate, then rest, loosely covered with foil, for 10 minutes.

Meanwhile, cook the kumara in a large saucepan of boiling water for 10 minutes or until tender. Drain, then return the kumara to the saucepan. Place over low heat, then add the milk and butter, season and mash until smooth. Keep warm.

For the three-mustard sauce, place the mayonnaise, creme fraiche, wholegrain mustard, Dijon mustard, wasabi and horseradish in a bowl and stir to combine. Season, then whisk in enough warm water to make a loose sauce. Set aside.

Slice the beef into thick pieces, then divide among plates and serve with the kumara mash, watercress and three-mustard sauce. Season with freshly ground black pepper and serve. **Serves 4**

Chicken, tomato & spinach curry

This recipe is inspired by my good friend Belinda Jeffery.
We worked together 20 years ago at Taylor's Restaurant in
Sydney and she remains one of my all-time favourite cooks.

¼ cup (60ml) olive oil

4 garlic cloves, chopped

2 tbs finely grated ginger

2 long red chillies, seeds
    removed, finely chopped

¼ cup (75g) tikka masala
    curry paste

6 skinless chicken
    thigh cutlets

3 (about 400g) potatoes,
    peeled, cut into 3cm cubes

400g can chopped tomatoes

12 fresh curry leaves*
    (optional)

1 cup (250ml) chicken stock

100g baby spinach leaves

Lime juice, to taste

Pappadams and steamed
    basmati rice, to serve

Heat the oil in a pan over medium heat. Add the garlic, ginger and chilli, and cook, stirring, for 1-2 minutes until fragrant. Add the curry paste and cook, stirring, for 2-3 minutes until fragrant. Add the chicken, turning to coat in the paste. Cook chicken for 1-2 minutes each side until lightly coloured, then add the potato, tomato, curry leaves and stock. Bring to a simmer, then reduce heat to medium-low, cover and cook for 15 minutes or until the chicken is cooked through and potato is tender.

Remove the lid and cook the curry for a further 20 minutes or until the sauce has thickened. Stir through the spinach and cook for a further 1-2 minutes until spinach has wilted. Add lime juice to taste and season. Serve the curry with pappadams and steamed basmati rice. **Serves 4-6**

* Fresh curry leaves are from Asian food shops and greengrocers.

Dirty rice with salmon

Dirty rice is a Cajun-inspired dish from America's Deep South.
Don't be put off by the name – this dish is packed with flavour.

¼ cup (60ml) olive oil

1 onion, sliced

2 garlic cloves,
   finely chopped

2 tsp ground coriander

2 tsp ground cumin

2 tsp ground turmeric

2 tsp paprika

1½ cups (300g) basmati rice

1L (4 cups) chicken stock
   (see 'Basics', p 296)

400g can chopped tomatoes

2 chorizo sausages, casings
   removed, chopped

225g jar El Navarrico
   Chargrilled Whole Piquillo
   Pimentos*, chopped

412g can black beans*,
   rinsed, drained

200g frozen peas,
   blanched, refreshed

1 bunch coriander,
   leaves picked

600g skinless salmon fillet,
   pin-boned

300g sour cream

Pinch of paprika

Preheat the oven to 190°C. Lightly grease a large baking tray.

Place 1 tablespoon olive oil in a saucepan over medium heat. Add the onion, garlic and 1 teaspoon each ground coriander, cumin, turmeric and paprika, then cook, stirring, for 3-4 minutes until softened. Add the rice, stirring to coat the grains, then add the stock and tomato. Bring to the boil, cover and reduce heat to low, then cook for 30 minutes, stirring occasionally, or until the stock has been absorbed and the rice is cooked.

Place 1 tablespoon oil in a frypan over medium heat. Cook chorizo, stirring, for 4-5 minutes until crispy. Remove with a slotted spoon and drain on paper towel. Add chorizo to the rice with the pimentos, beans, and peas, then stir over medium-low heat to warm through. Roughly chop half the coriander leaves and stir through the rice.

Meanwhile, place fish on the baking tray. In a small bowl, combine remaining 1 tablespoon oil with remaining spices, then season. Brush the spice mixture over the fish. Season with salt, then bake the fish for 15-20 minutes until just cooked through.

Spread the rice onto a serving platter. Using a fork, flake the salmon into large chunks, then arrange over the rice. Scatter with remaining coriander and serve with sour cream sprinkled with paprika. **Serves 6-8**

* El Navarrico Piquillo Pimentos are preserved chargrilled peppers from Spain, available from Simon Johnson (simonjohnson.com.au); substitute roast capsicum strips. Black beans are available from delis.

Herb-rubbed lamb cutlets with pea & feta salad

1 tbs whole black
  peppercorns
2 garlic cloves
2 long red chillies, seeds
  removed, finely chopped
2 tbs thyme leaves
2 tbs chopped sage leaves
2 tbs chopped
  flat-leaf parsley
¼ cup (60ml) olive oil
12 French-trimmed
  lamb cutlets
1 tsp Dijon mustard
1 tsp honey
Finely grated zest
  and juice of 1 lemon
½ cup (125ml) extra virgin
  olive oil

Pea & feta salad
250g small snow peas,
  trimmed
250g sugar snap peas,
  trimmed
200g frozen baby peas
2 cups mint leaves
200g marinated feta,
  drained

Place peppercorns, garlic, half the chilli and 1 teaspoon salt in a mortar and pestle and pound until coarsely ground. Add herbs and pound into a coarse paste. Stir in the olive oil and transfer to a large bowl. Add the lamb, turning to coat well in the herb marinade. Cover, then stand at room temperature for 30 minutes.

Preheat a chargrill pan or barbecue to medium-high heat.

Cook the lamb for 2-3 minutes each side for medium-rare or until cooked to your liking. Rest, loosely covered with foil, for 5 minutes.

Meanwhile, for the pea and feta salad, blanch the snow peas, sugar snap peas and baby peas in boiling salted water for 3 minutes or until just tender. Drain, then refresh in cold water. Transfer to a serving platter and top with mint leaves and feta.

Combine Dijon mustard, honey, lemon zest and juice, and remaining chilli, then slowly whisk in extra virgin olive oil. Season.

Arrange the lamb cutlets on top of the pea and feta salad, drizzle with the honey dressing and serve. **Serves 4**

Tuna with green tea noodles and black vinegar dressing

400g centre-cut
sashimi-grade tuna*
200g green tea noodles*
2 cups (300g) frozen, podded
edamame beans (young
green soy beans)*
1 bunch coriander,
leaves picked
Black sesame seeds*,
to serve

Black vinegar dressing
¾ cup (180ml) mirin
(Japanese rice wine)*
150ml yellow bean sauce*
or light soy sauce
⅓ cup (80ml) black vinegar*
⅓ cup (75g) caster sugar
2 tbs grated ginger
4 garlic cloves,
finely chopped
3 small red chillies,
seeds removed,
very finely chopped
1 tsp sesame oil

For the black vinegar dressing, combine the mirin, yellow bean sauce, black vinegar and caster sugar in a saucepan with 150ml cold water. Place over medium heat, stirring until sugar has dissolved. Add the ginger, garlic and chilli, then simmer for 5 minutes or until slightly reduced. Stir in the sesame oil, then set aside to cool.

Cut the tuna into 3cm cubes and toss with half the cooled dressing. Cover and allow to marinate in the fridge for 30 minutes.

Meanwhile, soak 8 wooden skewers in cold water for 30 minutes.

Cook the green tea noodles according to the packet instructions, adding the edamame for the final 1 minute of cooking time. Drain, refresh in cold water and set aside.

Preheat a chargrill pan or barbecue to medium-high heat.

Thread the tuna onto the soaked skewers. Grill the tuna for 2 minutes each side or until lightly charred on the outside, but still pink in the centre.

Toss the noodles and edamame with the coriander leaves and remaining dressing, then divide among bowls. Top with tuna skewers, sprinkle with black sesame seeds and serve. **Serves 4**

* Sashimi-grade tuna is available from fishmongers. Green tea noodles, edamame beans, black sesame seeds, mirin, yellow bean sauce and black vinegar are available from Asian food shops.

Print off some menus,
        lay out a white tablecloth
and add a touch of
restaurant chic to your home.

Spicy fish with Arabic orange & nasturtium salad

1 tsp chilli powder

1 tsp ground cumin

1 tsp ground cinnamon

100ml extra virgin olive oil

4 x 180g skinless white fish
fillets (such as blue-eye)

1 tbs caster sugar

2 tbs pomegranate
molasses*

2 oranges

6 radishes, sliced

¼ cup (35g) slivered
pistachios*

1 cup (120g) black olives

Watercress sprigs and
nasturtium flowers
and leaves*, to serve

Combine ½ tsp each chilli, cumin and cinnamon with 1 tablespoon oil
and 1 teaspoon salt to form a paste. Coat the fish in the spice mixture.

Heat 1 tablespoon olive oil in a frypan over medium heat. Cook the
fish for 2-3 minutes each side until golden and cooked through. Rest,
loosely covered with foil, while you prepare the dressing and salad.

In a bowl, combine the sugar, pomegranate molasses and remaining
spices and ¼ cup (60ml) olive oil. Whisk together until the sugar has
dissolved and set aside.

Peel and remove the white pith from oranges, then slice into thin
rounds and arrange on 4 plates. Scatter over the radish, pistachios,
olives and watercress.

To serve, top each plate with a piece of fish, garnish with the
nasturtium flowers and leaves and drizzle with the dressing. **Serves 4**

* Pomegranate molasses and slivered pistachios are available from
gourmet food shops and Middle Eastern food shops. Nasturtiums are
available from garden centres.

Pork chops with wild mushroom sauce and balsamic potatoes

⅓ cup (80ml) olive oil

1kg chat potatoes, halved

4 small red onions,
    halved or quartered

1 garlic bulb,
    halved horizontally

⅔ cup (160ml) balsamic
    vinegar

½ cup sage leaves,
    roughly chopped

125g unsalted butter

10g dried porcini
    mushrooms *

4 x 200g pork cutlets

150g mixed wild mushrooms
    (such as chestnuts, morels
    and chanterelles), halved
    or sliced if large

¾ cup (185ml) dry Marsala
    (Sicilian fortified wine)

½ cup (125ml) beef
    consomme

2 tbs chopped flat-leaf
    parsley, plus extra
    sprigs to serve

Preheat the oven to 180°C.

Heat 2 tablespoons olive oil in a large ovenproof frypan over medium heat. Season the potatoes and cook, cut-side down, for 10 minutes until golden and crispy. Add the onion, garlic, balsamic vinegar, sage and half the butter. Season, then transfer to the oven to cook for 25 minutes, turning once, or until vegetables are tender and caramelised.

Meanwhile, soak the porcini in ½ cup (125ml) boiling water for 10 minutes. Drain, reserving the soaking liquid, then roughly chop the porcini and set aside.

Place 1 tablespoon olive oil in a clean frypan over medium heat. Season the pork and cook for 5-6 minutes each side until golden and cooked through. Transfer to a plate and rest, loosely covered with foil, while you make the sauce.

Return frypan to medium-high heat and add remaining 1 tablespoon oil. Add the wild mushrooms and chopped porcini to the pan, season and cook, stirring, for 3-4 minutes until softened. Remove mushrooms from the pan and set aside. Add the Marsala, consomme and reserved soaking liquid to the pan. Bring to a simmer and cook for 5-6 minutes until reduced. Return the mushrooms to the pan. Chop the remaining butter into small pieces, then gradually whisk the butter into the sauce until it is thick and glossy.

Divide the pork among serving plates, drizzle with the sauce and scatter with chopped parsley. Garnish the balsamic roasted potatoes with parsley sprigs, then serve with the pork. **Serves 4**

* Dried porcini are available from gourmet food shops and delis.

Caramel raspberry tarts with orange cream

These tarts remind me of sweet little pizzas. They're the perfect note to finish your pop-up dinner party on with a home-brewed espresso or a glass of dessert wine.

3 sheets frozen puff pastry,
   thawed
100g brown sugar
50g unsalted butter
300ml thickened cream
2 x 125g punnets
   fresh raspberries
2 tbs icing sugar, sifted
Finely grated zest
   of 1 orange

Preheat the oven to 200°C. Line a baking tray with baking paper.

Using a 10cm round pastry cutter, cut the pastry into 6 rounds. Place pastry rounds on the baking tray and prick with a fork. Place another sheet of baking paper on top and weigh down the pastry with a heavy baking tray. Bake for 25 minutes or until pastry is golden.

Meanwhile, place the brown sugar, butter and ¼ cup (60ml) cream in a frypan over low heat. Cook, stirring, for 3-4 minutes until the sugar has dissolved and the sauce is a golden caramel.

Arrange raspberries on the cooked pastry rounds and generously brush with the caramel sauce. Bake tarts for 5-6 minutes until the sauce is bubbling, but the raspberries are still holding their shape. Cool to room temperature.

Place the icing sugar, orange zest and remaining cream in a bowl and whisk until soft peaks form. Serve the raspberry tarts with the orange cream. **Makes 6**

Black Forest Eton mess

680g jar pitted morello
  cherries
¼ cup (55g) caster sugar
150g dark chocolate,
  chopped
300ml thickened cream
2 tbs icing sugar, sifted
2 tbs kirsch*
6 store-bought meringues

Drain the cherries, reserving the juice. Place the cherry juice and caster sugar in a saucepan over low heat and cook, stirring, until the sugar has dissolved. Increase heat to medium-high and simmer for 4-5 minutes until reduced to about 1 cup (250ml). Remove from heat, then add the chocolate and stir until sauce is smooth. Set aside to cool.

Combine the cream and icing sugar in a bowl and whisk until soft peaks form. Stir in the kirsch and set aside.

Roughly crumble the meringues. Divide half the meringue among 8 serving glasses, then top with half the whipped cream and half the cherries. Repeat the layers, then drizzle over the chocolate cherry sauce and serve. **Serves 8**

* Kirsch is a clear, unsweetened cherry brandy, from bottleshops.

Rhubarb & strawberry crumbles

Add a little interest to dessert by serving these crumbles in cleaned cans.

1 bunch rhubarb, trimmed,
   cut into 3cm lengths
¼ cup (55g) caster sugar
2 tsp finely grated orange
   zest, plus ½ cup (125ml)
   orange juice
2 tsp cornflour
250g punnet strawberries,
   hulled, quartered
Pure (thin) cream, to serve

Crumble topping
100g unsalted butter
½ cup (110g) caster sugar
⅔ cup (100g) plain flour,
   sifted
⅔ cup (100g) pistachio
   kernels

Preheat the oven to 180°C. Line a baking tray with baking paper.

For the crumble topping, place the butter, sugar, flour and pistachios in a food processor and pulse until mixture resembles coarse crumbs. Spread onto the lined tray and refrigerate while you make the filling.

Place the rhubarb, sugar and orange zest and juice in a saucepan over medium-low heat. Cook, stirring, for 5 minutes or until just tender. Combine the cornflour with 1 tablespoon cold water, stirring to dissolve, then add to the pan. Cook, stirring, for 1-2 minutes until slightly thickened, then stir in the strawberries.

Divide the rhubarb mixture among six 1-cup (250ml) cleaned cans or ramekin dishes. Sprinkle over the crumble topping, then bake for 20 minutes or until topping is golden and the strawberries have released all their juices.

Drizzle the crumbles with cream and serve. **Makes 6**

Life's a beach

Summer is the sand between your toes and the sun on your back. It's the season of easy holiday food, lazy breakfasts, long lunches and fresh, zingy flavours that can be enjoyed at any time of the day.

Prawn & taramasalata rice paper rolls

Rice paper rolls are reinvented with creamy taramasalata and preserved lemon.

50g rice vermicelli noodles
12 round rice paper sheets*
   (20cm in diameter)
100g taramasalata*
½ Lebanese cucumber,
   cut into 12 thin batons
12 cooked prawns, peeled,
   deveined, halved
   lengthways
1 preserved lemon quarter*,
   white pith removed,
   rind thinly sliced
½ cup mint leaves,
   plus extra to serve
Lemon wedges, to serve

Lemon oil dressing
¼ cup (60ml) lemon-infused
   olive oil*
3 tsp lemon juice
½ tsp caster sugar

For the lemon oil dressing, whisk the oil, lemon juice and sugar together and season. Set aside.

Cook the vermicelli noodles according to packet instructions, then drain and rinse under cold water. Set aside.

Fill a large, shallow bowl with hot water. Dip 1 rice paper sheet in the water for 30 seconds or until softened. Remove from the water, then place on a damp tea towel and stand for 30 seconds until opaque and a little drier, but still pliable. Spread a little taramasalata along the centre of the rice paper, then top with a few vermicelli noodles, a cucumber baton, 2 prawn halves, a little preserved lemon rind and a few mint leaves. Fold the bottom edge of the rice paper over the filling, then fold in the sides and roll up to enclose. Cover with a damp tea towel, then repeat with the remaining ingredients to make 12 rolls.

Garnish the rolls with a few extra mint leaves and serve with the lemon oil dressing and lemon wedges. **Makes 12**

* Rice paper sheets are available from Asian food shops and selected supermarkets. Taramasalata, preserved lemon quarters and lemon-infused olive oil are available from gourmet food shops and delis.

Squid with chilli lime salt and homemade chilli jam

4 squid tubes, with tentacles
Sunflower oil, to deep-fry
2 eggwhites
½ cup (100g) rice flour

Chilli jam
2 tomatoes, chopped
1 cup (220g) caster sugar
4 long red chillies,
  roughly chopped
¼ cup (60ml) white vinegar
2 tbs lime juice
1 garlic clove, finely chopped
1 tbs fish sauce

Chilli lime salt
2 tsp dried chilli flakes
2 tbs caster sugar
⅓ cup (20g) fried Asian
  shallots *
Finely grated zest of 1 lime
2 tbs sea salt

Begin the chilli jam a day ahead.

For the chilli jam, place the tomato and sugar in a bowl, cover and stand at room temperature overnight. The next day, place the tomato mixture and chilli in a food processor and pulse to combine. Transfer to a saucepan over low heat and add the vinegar, lime juice, garlic and fish sauce, stirring to dissolve the sugar. Increase the heat to medium and simmer, stirring occasionally, for 15-20 minutes until thick and jammy. Set aside to cool.

For the chilli lime salt, place all ingredients in a mini food processor or a mortar and pestle and crush into a powder. Set aside.

Separate the squid tubes from the tentacles. Clean the squid tubes, then remove and discard the beaks from the tentacles. Slice the squid tubes lengthways to open up, then lightly score the inside. Cut into 2cm-wide strips. Set aside.

Half-fill a deep-fryer or large saucepan with oil and heat to 190°C (a cube of bread will turn golden in 30 seconds).

Lightly whisk the eggwhites in a bowl until frothy. Place the flour in a separate shallow bowl and season. Dip the squid tubes and tentacles first in the eggwhite, then in the flour, shaking off any excess. In batches, deep-fry the squid for 1 minute or until crispy – be careful not to overcook or the squid will become tough. Remove with a slotted spoon and drain on paper towel.

Sprinkle the fried squid pieces with the chilli lime salt and serve with the chilli jam. **Serves 4-6**

* Fried Asian shallots are available from Asian food shops and selected supermarkets.

Crab, coconut & green mango salad

1 green mango*, peeled
1 cup mint leaves
1 cup coriander leaves
2 kaffir lime leaves*,
 inner stem removed,
 very finely shredded
1½ tsp pickled ginger,
 thinly sliced
250g fresh crabmeat*
¼ cup (15g) shredded
 coconut, toasted
⅓ cup (50g) chopped
 roasted peanuts

Dressing
2 garlic cloves
1 small red chilli, seeds
 removed, finely chopped
1½ tbs fish sauce
2 tbs lime juice
1 tbs palm sugar*
2 tbs extra virgin olive oil

For the dressing, place garlic and chilli in a mortar and pestle, then pound to a coarse paste. Add the fish sauce, lime juice and sugar and stir to dissolve the sugar. Whisk in the olive oil and set aside.

Finely shred the mango (a mandoline is ideal), then place in a bowl with the mint, coriander, kaffir lime, ginger, crabmeat, coconut and peanuts.

To serve, drizzle the dressing over the salad and toss to combine. **Serves 4**

* Green mango, kaffir lime leaves and palm sugar are available from Asian food shops. Fresh crabmeat is available from fishmongers.

Grown-up chicken nuggets

Chicken nuggets shouldn't just be for the kids. This
sophisticated version will be equally popular with adults.

2 x 170g skinless chicken
   breast fillets
4 garlic cloves,
   finely chopped
¼ cup flat-leaf parsley
2 tbs chives
Finely grated zest
   of ½ lemon
3 eggs
2 cups (100g) panko
   breadcrumbs*
⅓ cup (50g) plain flour
Sunflower oil, to deep-fry
Aioli (see 'Basics', p 296) and
   shoestring fries, to serve

Roughly chop the chicken and place in a food processor with the
garlic, parsley, chives and zest, then season. Separate 1 egg, then
add the eggwhite to the chicken mixture, reserving the yolk, and
pulse to a coarse paste – be careful not to over-process. Divide the
mixture into 16 portions, then use damp hands to shape into nuggets.

Lightly beat 2 eggs and reserved yolk together in a separate bowl.
Place the panko breadcrumbs in a food processor and pulse to fine
crumbs, then transfer to a separate bowl. Place the flour in a third bowl
and season. Dip the nuggets first in the flour, then in the egg, then coat
in the panko crumbs. Cover and chill for 30 minutes.

Preheat the oven to 180°C. Half-fill a deep-fryer or large saucepan
with oil and heat to 190°C (a cube of bread will turn golden in 30 seconds).

In batches, deep-fry the nuggets for 3-4 minutes until golden.
Remove with a slotted spoon, drain on paper towel, then transfer to
the oven and bake for 5 minutes or until cooked through.

Serve the chicken nuggets with aioli and shoestring fries. **Serves 4**

* Panko breadcrumbs are available from Asian food shops
and selected supermarkets.

Prawns with tomato ice cream

It's quirky, I know, but savoury ice cream is a great way to start a meal in summer.

500g vine-ripened tomatoes
200ml thickened cream
1 tsp Worcestershire sauce
1½ tbs tomato paste
2 tsp caster sugar
1 small butter lettuce,
   leaves separated
18 cooked prawns, peeled
   (tails intact), deveined
¼ cup (50g) salmon roe
Basil leaves, to serve

Grate the tomatoes on the coarse side of a box grater and discard the skin. Press the grated tomatoes through a sieve, discarding the solids – you should have about 300ml tomato puree.

Whip the cream to soft peaks, then stir in the tomato puree, Worcestershire sauce, tomato paste and sugar. Season well.

Churn in an ice cream machine, according to manufacturer's instructions. Transfer to a plastic container and freeze for 3 hours or until firm.

To serve, divide the lettuce and prawns among serving bowls. Add a scoop of ice cream to each bowl, scatter with the salmon roe and basil leaves, then serve immediately. **Serves 4-6**

In my dreams I have a beautiful house
surrounded by *sand and sea*.

It's a lamb wrap

2 tbs extra virgin olive oil

2 tbs chopped oregano

2 garlic cloves,
    finely chopped

2 x 250g lamb backstraps,
    trimmed

4 spring onions, thinly sliced
    on the diagonal

120g marinated feta,
    drained, crumbled

⅓ cup (50g) pitted
    kalamata olives,
    roughly chopped

2 preserved lemon quarters*,
    white pith removed,
    rind thinly sliced

¼ cup (60g) semi-dried
    tomatoes, chopped

1 cup mint leaves

100g rocket

4 slices of mountain bread*

Combine the oil, oregano and garlic in a bowl. Coat the lamb in the marinade, cover and stand for 30 minutes.

Preheat the oven to 190°C.

Heat an ovenproof frypan over medium-high heat. Season the lamb, then cook for 2 minutes each side to seal. Transfer to the oven and bake for 5 minutes for medium-rare. Remove from the oven and rest, loosely covered with foil, for 5 minutes.

Thinly slice the lamb, then place in a bowl with the spring onion, feta, olives, preserved lemon rind, semi-dried tomato and mint and gently toss to combine.

Place rocket on the mountain bread, top with the lamb and feta salad, then roll up and serve. **Makes 4**

* Preserved lemon quarters are available from gourmet food shops and delis. Mountain bread is available from supermarkets.

Crisp pork belly with sour peach salad

The sour peaches in this salad help cut through the richness of the pork.

1kg boneless pork belly
   (skin on)
3 garlic cloves, grated
2 tbs light soy sauce
2 tbs olive oil
½ tsp chilli flakes
1 tsp five spice

Sour peach salad
1 tbs peanut oil
⅓ cup (80ml) lime juice
1 garlic clove, crushed
1 small red chilli, seeds
   removed, finely chopped
1 tbs palm sugar*
1 tbs fish sauce
1 tbs light soy sauce
2 tbs toasted chopped
   macadamias
4 eschalots, thinly sliced
2 cups mixed fresh herbs
   (such as Thai basil*,
   coriander and mint)
3 slightly under-ripe
   peaches, cut into wedges

Score the pork belly skin in a crisscross pattern. Place pork on a rack in the sink and pour over a kettle of boiling water (this will result in crisp crackling). Pat dry with paper towel.

Combine garlic, soy sauce, oil, chilli and five spice in a bowl with 2 teaspoons sea salt. Rub marinade into pork skin. Cover and refrigerate for at least 4 hours or overnight.

The next day, preheat the oven to 220°C.

Place the pork on a rack in a roasting pan, skin-side up. Pour enough boiling water to fill the pan to just below the rack and roast for 30 minutes or until the skin is crispy. Reduce temperature to 180°C and cook for a further 1½ hours or until the meat is tender. Rest, loosely covered with foil, for 10 minutes.

For the sour peach salad, combine the oil, lime juice, garlic, chilli, sugar, fish sauce and soy sauce in a bowl, stirring to dissolve the sugar. Place the macadamias, eschalot, herbs and peach in a bowl. Drizzle over most of the dressing and toss to combine.

Carve the pork, drizzle with the remaining dressing and serve with the sour peach salad. **Serves 6-8**

* Palm sugar and Thai basil are available from Asian food shops.

Peach Melba buttermilk puddings

5 titanium-strength
  gelatine leaves*
600ml thickened cream
1 cup (220g) caster sugar
2 tsp vanilla extract
400ml buttermilk
4 ripe yellow peaches
2 x 125g punnets
  raspberries

Soak 3 gelatine leaves in cold water for 5 minutes to soften.

Place the cream, sugar, vanilla and buttermilk in a saucepan over medium heat, stirring to dissolve the sugar. Squeeze excess water from the gelatine, then add the gelatine to the cream mixture, stirring to dissolve. Strain the mixture through a fine sieve into a jug, then cool slightly and pour into 6 serving glasses. Cover and refrigerate for 3 hours or until set.

Meanwhile, cut a small cross in the base of each peach and place in a bowl. Pour in enough boiling water to cover the fruit and stand for 1 minute. Drain, then peel the peaches. Chop the peach flesh, discarding the stones. Place the flesh in a blender and puree until smooth, then pass through a sieve, dressing down to extract the juice. Discard the solids and set the peach puree aside.

Meanwhile, soak the remaining 2 gelatine leaves in cold water for 5 minutes to soften. Warm the peach puree in a saucepan over low heat. Squeeze excess water from the gelatine, then add the gelatine to the puree. Remove from heat and stir to dissolve the gelatine.

Cool, then pour the puree over the set buttermilk puddings and refrigerate for a further 2 hours or until set.

Garnish puddings with the raspberries and serve. **Makes 6**

* Gelatine leaves are available from gourmet food shops.

Mango risotto with tropical fruit

Risotto for breakfast is a summertime treat and a decadent
way to start the day with seasonal fruit.

½ cup (110g) caster sugar
1 vanilla bean, split,
  seeds scraped
2 star anise
1 tbs finely grated
  lemon zest
1 tbs finely grated
  orange zest
25g unsalted butter
1 cup (220g) arborio rice
2 mangoes, chopped
150ml coconut cream,
  plus extra to serve
Tropical fruit and toasted
  coconut flakes, to serve

Place the sugar in a saucepan over low heat with the vanilla pod and
seeds, star anise, citrus zest and 1L (4 cups) water. Stir to dissolve
the sugar. Increase heat to medium-low and simmer for 5 minutes.

In a separate saucepan, melt the butter over low heat and add
the rice, stirring for 1 minute to coat the grains. Add the sugar
syrup and simmer for 30-40 minutes, stirring occasionally, until
the rice is al dente. Cool slightly.

Meanwhile, place the mango flesh in a food processor and process until
a smooth puree. Stir the puree and coconut cream through the risotto.

Serve the mango risotto warm or chilled with the tropical fruit. Drizzle
with extra coconut cream and garnish with coconut flakes. **Serves 4-6**

Watermelon mojito ice blocks

1 cup (250ml) sugar syrup
  (see 'Basics', p 296)
1 cup mint leaves
700g peeled watermelon,
  chopped
3 titanium-strength
  gelatine leaves*
1 cup (250ml) white rum
Juice of 3 limes

Begin this recipe a day ahead.

Place the sugar syrup and ½ cup mint leaves in a saucepan over medium heat and simmer for 2-3 minutes. Remove from the heat and stand for 30 minutes to infuse.

Meanwhile, place the watermelon in a blender and puree until smooth. Pass through a sieve pressing down on the solids to extract all the juice – you should have about 2 cups (500ml) puree. Set aside.

Soak the gelatine leaves in cold water for 5 minutes until softened. Strain the infused sugar syrup into a saucepan, discarding the mint leaves, and simmer over high heat for 1 minute. Squeeze out any excess water from the gelatine leaves, then add the gelatine to the sugar syrup, stirring to dissolve. Allow to cool slightly, then stir in the rum, lime juice and watermelon puree.

Pour the watermelon mojito mixture into ice-block moulds, then divide the remaining ½ cup mint leaves among the moulds. Freeze overnight or until completely frozen. **Makes about 15**

* Gelatine leaves are available from gourmet food shops.

A moveable feast

Why does food taste so much better at a picnic?
Probably because it's an adventure loved by all the
family. So pack the hamper and rug – let's eat outside.

Garlic prawn pâté

200g unsalted butter

350g peeled green prawns

3 garlic cloves, chopped

¼ tsp freshly grated nutmeg

1 tsp finely grated
lemon zest, plus ¼ cup
(60ml) lemon juice

2 tbs whole-egg mayonnaise

2 tbs chopped dill, plus
a few extra sprigs to serve

1 baguette

Extra virgin olive oil,
to brush

Melt 100g butter in a frypan over medium heat. Season the prawns, then add to the pan with the garlic and cook, stirring, for 3-4 minutes until prawns are cooked through. Cool completely.

Transfer the cooled prawn mixture to a food processor with the nutmeg and lemon zest and juice. Whiz until a smooth paste, then add the mayonnaise and chopped dill and pulse a few times until combined. Season, then divide the mixture among 4 small ramekins or teacups, smoothing the tops with the back of a spoon. Set aside.

Melt the remaining 100g butter in a pan until foaming. Cool slightly, then skim the surface of the butter with a spoon, discarding any white solids. Top each pâté with the clarified butter and a dill sprig, then place in the refrigerator for 30 minutes or until set.

Preheat oven to 180°C and line a baking tray with baking paper.

Cut the baguette into 1cm-thick slices on the diagonal. Lightly brush the bread slices on one side with olive oil, arrange on the lined tray and bake for 20 minutes until crisp and golden. Remove from the tray and set aside to cool. Serve the pâté with the baguette croutons. The pâtés will keep in the refrigerator for up to 5 days. **Serves 8**

Beef carpaccio with beetroot and sauce gribiche

This recipe is inspired by Alla Wolf-Tasker from Lake House in Daylesford, Victoria. A passionate campaigner for sustainable, regional produce, Alla is truly one of Australia's great food heroes. I hope she won't mind me sharing a cheat's version of her sauce gribiche.

500g piece centre-cut
    beef eye fillet, trimmed
3 baby beetroots*,
    trimmed, peeled
1 tbs red wine vinegar
2 tbs extra virgin olive oil

Sauce gribiche
1 cup (300g) whole-egg
    mayonnaise
1 tbs finely chopped tarragon
1 tbs finely chopped dill
1 tbs finely chopped
    flat-leaf parsley
1 tbs capers, rinsed, drained
1 tbs Dijon mustard
1 eschalot, finely chopped

Season the beef, then enclose tightly in plastic wrap and place in the freezer for 20 minutes until firm. Remove the plastic wrap and thinly slice the beef. Place each slice between 2 sheets of baking paper and flatten gently with a rolling pin. Refrigerate until ready to serve.

Meanwhile, cut the beetroot into thin slices (a mandoline is ideal). Cut into thin matchsticks. Whisk the vinegar and oil together, season well, then toss with the beetroot. Set aside.

For the sauce gribiche, combine all ingredients in a bowl and season. Set aside.

Bring the beef to room temperature, then arrange on a serving platter. Scatter over the beetroot, drizzle with the sauce gribiche and serve. **Serves 6-8**

* We used a selection of heirloom beetroots which are available in a range of colours from farmers' markets and selected greengrocers.

Hot-smoked trout & rice salad with mint pesto

1 cup (200g) long-grain rice
1½ cups fresh or frozen peas
2 firmly packed cups mint
    leaves, plus extra to serve
½ firmly packed cup
    basil leaves
¾ cup (60g) finely grated
    parmesan
25g pine nuts, toasted
¼ cup (60ml) lemon juice
1 garlic clove, chopped
⅓ cup (80ml) olive oil
2 x 150g hot-smoked trout
    portions*, flaked

Cook the rice according to the packet instructions, then drain and refresh. Spread the rice on a baking tray to cool completely.

Cook the peas in boiling salted water for 2-3 minutes until tender. Drain, refresh and set aside.

Place the mint, basil, parmesan, pine nuts, lemon juice, garlic, ½ cup peas, and ½ teaspoon sea salt in a food processor and whiz until smooth. With the motor running, slowly drizzle in oil until combined, then season to taste.

Toss the rice with the remaining 1 cup peas and serve with the pesto, flaked trout and extra mint leaves, to garnish. **Serves 4-6**

✱ Hot-smoked trout portions are available from supermarkets.

Roasted tomato soup

1.5kg vine-ripened
  tomatoes, halved
2 onions, quartered
¼ cup (60ml) extra
  virgin olive oil
3 garlic cloves, chopped
2 tsp finely grated ginger
1 small red chilli, seeds
  removed, finely chopped
300ml tomato juice
800ml coconut milk
1 small bunch coriander,
  leaves and stems finely
  chopped, plus extra
  whole leaves to serve
1 tbs brown sugar
2 tbs fish sauce
Natural yoghurt and
  warm roti, to serve

Preheat the oven to 180°C. Line a baking tray with foil.

Place the tomato and onion on the baking tray and drizzle with 2 tablespoons olive oil. Season and roast for 1½ hours or until tomato and onion are very soft and lightly charred.

Meanwhile, heat remaining 1 tablespoon oil in a saucepan over medium heat. Cook the garlic, ginger and chilli, stirring, for 1-2 minutes until fragrant. Add the tomato juice, coconut milk and chopped coriander leaves and stems, then simmer for 6-8 minutes. Add the sugar, fish sauce, roasted tomato and onion, plus any cooking juices. Simmer for a further 2 minutes or until slightly thickened, remove from heat and allow to cool slightly.

Transfer the tomato mixture to a blender and blend until smooth. Season to taste.

Serve the soup either chilled or warm. Garnish the soup with coriander leaves, drizzle with yoghurt and serve with roti. **Serves 6-8**

Still-life tart

This pretty-as-a-picture goat's cheese tart will be a real talking point. Feel free to vary the topping with whatever vegetables and herbs you have on hand.

1 king mushroom
1 spring onion
2 tsp olive oil
1 cup (250g) mascarpone
150g soft goat's cheese
20g unsalted butter, softened
3 eggs
300ml thickened cream
About 10 enoki mushrooms
3 dill sprigs

Pastry
1⅔ cups (250g) plain flour
125g chilled unsalted butter, chopped
2 egg yolks

For the pastry, place flour and butter in a food processor with ½ teaspoon salt and whiz until fine crumbs. Add egg yolks and ¼ cup (60ml) iced water. Process until the mixture comes together in a smooth ball. Enclose in plastic wrap and chill for 30 minutes.

Lightly grease a 27cm x 19cm loose-bottomed tart pan. Roll the pastry out on a lightly floured surface until 5mm thick, then use it to line the tart pan. Chill for a further 30 minutes.

Preheat the oven to 180°C.

Line the pastry case with baking paper and fill with pastry weights or uncooked rice. Bake for 10 minutes, then remove weights and paper and bake for a further 3 minutes until pastry is golden and dry. Set aside.

Slice the king mushroom lengthways and place on a baking tray with the spring onion. Brush with the oil and roast for 5-6 minutes until the spring onion begins to wilt. Set aside.

Meanwhile, place mascarpone, goat's cheese, butter, eggs and cream in a food processor and whiz until smooth. Season, then pour into the tart case and bake for 10 minutes or until just starting to set. Arrange the king and enoki mushrooms, spring onion and dill sprigs on top of the tart and bake for a further 15 minutes or until the filling is set. Serve warm. **Serves 4-6**

Don't limit eating outside to
summer – it's a pleasure
to be enjoyed all year around.
Happy days.

Beetroot & goat's cheese jalousie

For a short-cut version, you can just use a jar of good-quality
store-bought beetroot marmalade with the goat's cheese for the filling.

2 beetroots

2 green apples,
    coarsely grated

¼ tsp freshly grated nutmeg

¼ tsp ground cloves

2 star anise

200ml red wine vinegar

150g caster sugar

2 x 375g blocks frozen
    puff pastry, thawed

300g marinated goat's
    cheese, drained

1 tbs thyme leaves

1 egg, lightly beaten

Creme fraiche, to serve

Preheat the oven to 180°C.

Enclose the beetroots in foil, then roast for 1 hour or until tender.
Cool, then peel and coarsely grate.

Place the grated beetroot and apple in a saucepan with the spices,
vinegar and sugar and bring to a simmer, stirring to dissolve the sugar.
Reduce the heat to medium, cover and cook for 1 hour or until thickened
and reduced. Remove the lid and cook for a further 8-10 minutes until
all the liquid has evaporated. Remove from heat and cool completely.

Preheat the oven to 190°C. Line a baking tray with baking paper.

Roll out 1 pastry block on a floured surface to form a 15cm x 35cm
rectangle. Place on the baking tray and spread the beetroot mixture
over the pastry rectangle leaving a 2cm border on all sides. Scatter
with goat's cheese and thyme leaves, then season.

Roll out the remaining pastry block into a rectangle slightly larger
than the first and fold in half lengthways. Use a sharp knife to make
cuts in the folded side about 1cm apart and leaving a 2cm border
on the unfolded side. Carefully open the pastry and place over the
filling, pressing to seal the edges. The cuts in the pastry should
separate slightly to reveal some of the filling.

Trim the edges of the jalousie, then brush all over with egg.
Place in the oven and bake for 25-30 minutes until puffed and
golden. Serve with creme fraiche. **Serves 4-6**

Jerk chicken

The fiery flavours of jerk seasoning come from the
Caribbean and make a welcome change to a roast chicken.

4 chicken drumsticks
(skin on)
4 chicken thigh cutlets
(skin on)
Lemon halves and mixed
salad leaves, to serve

Jerk marinade
1 onion, chopped
2 red chillies, seeds
removed, chopped
2 garlic cloves, chopped
4cm-piece fresh ginger,
chopped
2 tsp thyme leaves
¼ tsp ground allspice
½ cup (125ml) cider vinegar
½ cup (125ml) soy sauce
1 tbs honey
⅓ cup (80ml) olive oil

For the marinade, place the onion, chilli, garlic, ginger and thyme
in a food processor and whiz until chopped. Add the allspice, vinegar,
soy sauce, honey and oil. Whiz until a thick paste.

Score in the flesh side of the chicken, then coat well in the
marinade. Cover and refrigerate for 3 hours or overnight.

Preheat the oven to 180°C. Place a wire rack over a roasting
pan filled with 2cm water.

Drain the chicken, reserving the marinade, then place the chicken on
the rack. Bake for 30 minutes, then brush with the reserved marinade.
Bake the chicken for a further 30 minutes or until cooked through.

Serve the jerk chicken hot or cold with lemon halves and mixed
salad leaves. **Serves 4-6**

Lemon & lime curd with fresh ricotta and blueberries

I love lemon curd. I always have a jar in the fridge for filling tarts, cakes and crepes – and for stealing spoonfuls to satisfy sweet cravings when nobody is looking!

Finely grated zest of
   2 lemons, plus juice
   of 1 lemon
Finely grated zest
   and juice of 2 limes
3 eggs, lightly beaten
100g unsalted
   butter, chopped
200g caster sugar
Fresh ricotta, blueberries
   and almond biscotti,
   to serve

Place the lemon and lime zests and juices in a heatproof bowl with the eggs, butter and sugar. Place the bowl over a saucepan of gently simmering water (don't let the bowl touch the water) and cook, stirring occasionally, for 20 minutes or until thickened. Cool slightly.

Pour curd into clean, sterilised jars. Cool completely, then cover and chill for 1 hour or until set.

Serve the curd with wedges of fresh ricotta, blueberries and biscotti.

Makes about 2 cups

Pimm's jellies with traditional garnish

Pimm's is the classic British summer drink. Its herbaceous flavour makes it a wonderful choice for a refreshing dessert, too.

⅓ cup (75g) caster sugar
1 bunch mint, leaves picked,
    plus extra leaves to serve
6 gold-strength
    gelatine leaves*
1 cup (250ml) Pimm's
    No. 1 Cup
2 cups (500ml) lemonade
Sliced orange, strawberries
    and cucumber, to serve

Place sugar and 1 cup (250ml) water in a saucepan over a low heat, stirring to dissolve the sugar. Remove from the heat, than add the mint leaves and stand for 30 minutes to infuse. Strain the syrup and discard the mint leaves.

Soak the gelatine leaves in cold water for 5 minutes.

Return the infused sugar syrup to medium heat. Squeeze the gelatine leaves of excess water, then add the gelatine to the pan, stirring to dissolve the gelatine. Remove from heat and allow to cool slightly.

Add the Pimm's and the lemonade to the syrup and strain into a jug. Pour into serving glasses, then cover and chill for 4 hours or until set.

Serve the Pimm's jellies with a traditional garnish of mint and slices of orange slices, strawberries and cucumber. **Makes 6**

✳ Gold-strength gelatine leaves are available from gourmet food shops.

Yoghurt cake with sangria-poached fruit

1 cup (280g) thick
   Greek-style yoghurt,
   plus extra to serve
1 cup (220g) caster sugar
1 tsp vanilla extract
⅓ cup (80ml) sunflower oil
2 eggs
1⅔ cups (250g) plain flour
1½ tsp baking powder
1 tsp baking soda
Finely grated zest of 1 lemon
Finely grated zest of 1 orange
Icing sugar, to dust

Sangria-poached fruit
3 cups (750ml) red wine
400g frozen mixed berries
½ cup (110g) caster sugar
1 vanilla bean, split,
   seeds scraped
Pared rind of ½ lemon
Pared rind of ½ orange
2 dark plums, halved, stoned
2 pears, cored, quartered
4 figs, halved
1 cup (150g) cherries

Preheat the oven to 170°C. Grease and line the base and sides of a 20cm round springform cake pan with baking paper.

Combine yoghurt, caster sugar and vanilla in a bowl and whisk until smooth. Whisk in the oil until well combined, then add the eggs, one at a time, beating well with a wooden spoon after each addition. Sift the flour, baking powder and baking soda into the bowl, then add the citrus zest and a pinch of salt and stir to combine.

Spread the cake batter into the prepared pan and bake for 45 minutes or until a skewer inserted in the centre comes out clean. (Cover loosely with foil if the cake is browning too quickly.) Allow to cool completely in the pan, then dust with icing sugar.

Meanwhile, for the sangria-poached fruit, place the wine, mixed berries and sugar in a saucepan over low heat, stirring to dissolve sugar. Bring to a simmer and cook for 10 minutes or until the berries are soft. Remove from the heat and stand for 30 minutes to allow flavours to infuse. Pass through a fine sieve, pressing down on the solids to extract the juices. Discard the solids, then return the liquid to the pan. Add vanilla pod and seeds and pared citrus rind to the liquid, then add the plums, pears, figs and cherries. Place over medium-low heat and bring to a simmer. Cook for 8 minutes or until the fruit is tender (the cooking time will vary depending on the ripeness of the pears). Serve the sangria-poached fruit warm or chilled with the yoghurt cake and extra yoghurt. **Serves 6-8**

Keeping up appearances

This chapter is about 'red carpet' dining – for those occasions when you need to pull out all the stops to impress family and friends. It could even be worth inventing a special event just to celebrate!

Scallops with cauliflower puree and crispy jamon crumbs

40g unsalted butter

2 tbs olive oil

4 thyme sprigs

2 slices jamon* or
  prosciutto, chopped

1 cup (70g) fresh sourdough
  breadcrumbs

¼ cup flat-leaf parsley
  leaves

2 cups (200g) small
  cauliflower florets

2 cups (500ml) milk

¼ tsp freshly grated nutmeg

16 large scallops
  on the half shell

Melt 20g butter with 1 tablespoon oil in a frypan over medium heat. Pick the leaves from 2 thyme sprigs and add the leaves to the frypan with the jamon and breadcrumbs. Cook, stirring, for 1-2 minutes until golden. Place the jamon mixture in a food processor with the parsley and pulse to coarse crumbs. Season and set aside.

Meanwhile, place the cauliflower, milk and remaining 2 thyme sprigs in a pan over medium heat. Bring to just below boiling point and cook for 10 minutes or until the cauliflower is tender. Drain, reserving the milk. Discard the thyme, then place the cauliflower in a food processor and whiz until smooth. With the motor running, gradually add enough of the reserved milk to make a smooth puree. Add the nutmeg and season. Keep warm and set aside.

Heat the remaining 20g butter and 1 tablespoon oil in a clean frypan over high heat. Season the scallops and cook for 1 minute each side or until golden but still translucent in the centre.

To serve, spoon some cauliflower puree onto each half shell, sit the scallops on top, then scatter with the jamon crumbs. **Serves 4**

* Jamon is a Spanish cured ham available from gourmet food shops and delis.

Corn soup with avocado, lime and grilled prawns

This recipe is inspired by Jimmy McIntyre from Otahuna Lodge
– one of my favourite places to visit in New Zealand.

6 corn cobs, kernels sliced
    (cobs reserved)
20g unsalted butter
⅓ cup (80ml) olive oil
1 onion, finely chopped
12 green prawns, peeled
    (tails intact), deveined
2 small avocados,
    finely chopped
Finely grated zest and
    juice of 1 lime
Paprika and chopped
    flat-leaf parsley, to serve
Avocado oil* or extra virgin
    olive oil, to drizzle

Place the corn cobs in a saucepan with 2L (8 cups) cold water over medium-high heat. Bring to the boil, then reduce heat to medium-low and simmer for 15 minutes. Strain and reserve the liquid. Discard cobs.

Heat butter and 2 tablespoons olive oil in a saucepan over medium-low heat. Add onion and cook for 6-8 minutes, stirring, until soft. Add corn kernels and cook for 5 minutes, stirring, until softened but not browned.

Add enough corn stock to cover and simmer over medium-high heat for 15 minutes or until corn is tender. Cool slightly, then blend, in batches, until smooth. Strain, season, then gently reheat in a clean saucepan over medium-low heat, adding a little more corn stock for a smooth consistency, if needed.

Meanwhile, heat the remaining 2 tablespoons olive oil in a frypan over medium-high heat. Season prawns and cook for 1 minute each side or until just cooked through.

Mix avocado and lime zest and juice together, then season.

To serve, divide soup among serving bowls, then top with prawns. Scatter over the avocado, sprinkle with paprika and parsley, and drizzle with avocado or extra virgin olive oil. **Serves 6**

* Avocado oil is available from selected supermarkets and delis.

Vodka-cured ocean trout with soy jelly

1kg centre-cut ocean trout
    fillet, pin-boned, skin on
1 vanilla bean, split,
    seeds scraped
¼ cup (60ml) vodka
½ cup (150g) rock salt
½ firmly packed cup (125g)
    brown sugar
2 gold-strength gelatine
    leaves*
½ cup (125ml) soy sauce
¼ cup (60ml) mirin
    (Japanese rice wine)*
½ avocado, finely chopped
50g salmon roe*
Dill sprigs, micro coriander
    sprigs* and aioli (see
    'Basics', p 296) , to serve

Begin this recipe a day ahead.

Place the fish, skin-side down, on a clean work surface and rub the flesh with vanilla seeds. Place the fish in a shallow dish, pour over the vodka, then cover and refrigerate for 1 hour.

Whiz the rock salt and sugar in a food processor until finely ground. Combine the vanilla pod with the salt mixture. Remove the fish from the fridge, rub the salt mixture onto the flesh, then cover and return to the fridge to chill overnight.

Meanwhile, place gelatine leaves in a bowl of cold water for 5 minutes or until softened.

Warm the soy sauce and mirin in a small saucepan over low heat. Squeeze excess water from the gelatine, then add the gelatine to the saucepan, stirring until dissolved. Strain into a shallow rectangular or square container. Cool, then chill overnight until the jelly has set.

The next day, rinse the fish in cold water and pat dry with paper towel. Carefully remove the skin using a sharp knife.

To serve, cut the fish into very thin slices and arrange on a serving platter. Cut the soy jelly into small cubes and scatter over the fish. Garnish with chopped avocado, roe and herbs. Loosen the aioli with a little water, then drizzle over the ocean trout. **Serves 8-10**

* Gelatine leaves are from gourmet food shops. Mirin is available from supermarkets and Asian food shops. Salmon roe is from delis and fishmongers. Micro coriander sprigs are available from selected greengrocers and farmers' markets.

Smoky Spanish chicken

80g unsalted butter

Finely grated zest
  of 2 oranges

2 garlic cloves,
  finely chopped

2 tsp smoked paprika
  (pimenton)

½ tsp chilli flakes

1½ cups (105g) fresh
  breadcrumbs

½ cup (60g) pitted black
  olives, chopped

¼ cup finely chopped
  flat-leaf parsley

4 x 170g skinless chicken
  breast fillets

¼ cup (60ml) olive oil

1 chorizo sausage, casing
  removed, finely chopped

Rocket leaves and
  orange wedges, to serve

Melt 50g butter and cool slightly. Combine the orange zest, garlic, paprika, chilli, breadcrumbs and olives with the melted butter and 2 tablespoons parsley. Season. Place the chicken on a clean board and carefully make a deep incision in the side of each fillet horizontally, being careful not to cut all the way through.

Stuff each fillet with the breadcrumb filling. Secure the fillets in four places with kitchen string. Enclose each one individually in plastic wrap, twisting the ends so it is tightly sealed, then secure the ends with kitchen string. Refrigerate for 1 hour.

Remove the chicken from the fridge and place in a steamer. Steam for 20 minutes or until almost cooked through.

Melt remaining 30g butter with the oil in a frypan over medium heat. Remove the chicken from the plastic wrap, season, then cook, turning, for 4-5 minutes until golden on all sides. Remove from the frypan, loosely cover with foil, then set aside to rest.

Return the frypan to medium heat and cook the chopped chorizo for 1-2 minutes until crispy. Set aside.

On a clean board, roll the chicken in the remaining 1 tablespoon parsley, then slice. Divide chicken among plates, sprinkle with the chorizo and drizzle with any pan juices. Serve with the rocket and orange wedges. **Serves 4**

Lobster Thermidor

This classic lobster dish is the ideal way to impress your guests.

1 cup (250ml) milk
1 onion, halved
2 fresh bay leaves*
2 cooked lobsters*
60g unsalted butter
30g plain flour
1 cup (250ml) white wine
¼ cup (60ml) thickened
  cream
3 spring onions,
  finely chopped
2 tsp Dijon mustard
2 tsp chopped tarragon
2 tsp chopped chives
100g gruyere cheese, grated
Dressed salad leaves,
  to serve

Place the milk, onion and bay leaves in a saucepan over medium heat and bring to just below boiling point. Remove from heat, then stand for 30 minutes to infuse. Strain the milk into a jug and set aside.

Meanwhile, halve the lobsters, scoop out the meat and roughly chop. Clean the half shells and place on a baking tray.

Melt the butter in a clean saucepan over low heat. Add the flour and cook, stirring, for 1 minute. Whisk in the white wine and cook, stirring, for 2-3 minutes, then add the infused milk, whisking constantly, for 5 minutes or until smooth and thickened. Stir in the cream, spring onion, mustard, herbs and half the cheese, then season. Stir in the lobster meat, then divide the mixture among the lobster shells. Scatter with the remaining 50g cheese.

Heat the grill to high. Grill the lobsters for 5-6 minutes until bubbling and golden. Serve with dressed salad leaves. **Serves 4**

* Fresh bay leaves are available from greengrocers. Cooked lobsters are available from fishmongers and selected supermarkets.

Don't forget to create
an oh-so-perfect setting
for a dinner party to remember.

Duck with cherry sauce

2 x 1.8kg whole ducks *
670g jar pitted morello
  cherries
Juice of 1 orange
1 cup (250ml) port
2 tbs caster sugar
2 cinnamon quills
250g jar redcurrant jelly
2 tsp cornflour
Watercress sprigs, to serve

Begin this recipe a day ahead.

Rinse the ducks in cold water, then pat dry with paper towel. Place the ducks in the refrigerator, uncovered, overnight. (This will allow them to dry out, which will ensure a golden, crispy skin.)

The next day, remove the ducks from the refrigerator and bring to room temperature.

Preheat the oven to 190°C.

Place the ducks in a roasting pan and season. Roast the ducks, removing from the oven every 30 minutes to carefully drain the fat, for 1½ hours or until cooked through and skin is crispy and golden. (The duck fat can be reserved and used to roast potatoes.) Remove the ducks from the oven and rest, loosely covered with foil, while you make the cherry sauce.

Drain the cherries, reserving the juice. Place the cherry juice, orange juice, port, sugar and cinnamon in a pan over medium-low heat, stirring to dissolve sugar, then simmer for 5-6 minutes until the sauce is reduced by half. Add the redcurrant jelly and stir until dissolved. Combine the cornflour with 2 tablespoons water, stirring until dissolved, then stir into the sauce with the cherries. Simmer for 2-3 minutes until the mixture has thickened.

To serve, carve each duck into 8 pieces and arrange on a large plate. Scatter with the watercress and serve with the cherry sauce. **Serves 4**

* Whole ducks are available from poultry shops and selected butchers.

Lamb tian

2 garlic cloves,
  finely chopped

2 tbs olive oil

1 tbs chopped rosemary
  leaves

2 x 250g lamb backstraps,
  trimmed

600ml jar good-quality
  tomato pasta sauce

8 slices chargrilled
  eggplant*

200g baby spinach, wilted,
  plus extra leaves to serve

12 slices chargrilled
  kumara*

250g punnet vine-ripened
  cherry tomatoes

⅓ cup (80ml) white wine

150ml beef consomme
  or demi-glaze*

Combine garlic, olive oil and rosemary in a bowl. Coat lamb in the mixture, cover and refrigerate for 30 minutes.

Meanwhile, preheat the oven to 200°C. Lightly grease four 8cm x 6cm ring moulds and place on a baking tray.

Place the tomato sauce in a saucepan over medium-low heat and cook, stirring occasionally, for 6-8 minutes until thickened. Set aside.

Divide the eggplant slices among the moulds and season. Top with the wilted spinach, then the kumara slices and finish with the tomato sauce, seasoning between each layer.

Place a frypan over medium-high heat. Add the lamb and cook, turning, for 4 minutes or until sealed on all sides. Transfer to a baking tray and bake for a further 8 minutes for medium-rare. Remove the lamb from the oven, and rest, loosely covered with foil, for 5 minutes.

Meanwhile, season the tomatoes, then place on the tray with the ring moulds. Roast for 6-8 minutes to warm through. Set aside.

Return the frypan to medium heat, add the white wine and simmer for 1-2 minutes. Add the consomme or demi-glaze and simmer for a further 3-4 minutes until reduced by half.

Using a fish slice, carefully transfer each ring mould to a plate. Thinly slice the lamb and divide among moulds, overlapping slightly in a circular pattern. Remove the ring moulds. Serve tians drizzled with the sauce and scattered with tomatoes and extra spinach leaves. **Serves 4**

* Chargrilled vegetables are available from delis. Demi-glaze is available from gourmet food shops.

Strawberry soup with goat's milk sorbet

4 x 250g punnets
    strawberries, hulled
½ cup (110g) caster sugar
Juice of ½ lemon
½ tsp arrowroot*
125g punnet raspberries

Goat's milk sorbet
2 cups (500ml) goat's milk*
125g caster sugar
3 vanilla beans, split,
    seeds scraped
150ml thickened cream,
    lightly whipped

For the sorbet, place milk, sugar and vanilla pods and seeds in a saucepan over medium heat and bring to just below boiling point. Remove from the heat, then stand for 30 minutes to infuse. Strain the mixture into a container and cool slightly. Cover and chill for 2 hours. Once cold, transfer sorbet to an ice cream machine and churn according to the manufacturer's instructions. Just before the sorbet has reached setting point, add the whipped cream, then churn for 1 minute to combine. Transfer the sorbet to a clean, shallow, airtight container and freeze until firm.

Meanwhile, combine the strawberries, sugar and lemon juice in a heatproof bowl. Cover with foil and place over a saucepan of barely simmering water. Simmer, topping up the saucepan with more water as needed, for 1 hour or until strawberries are very soft.

Pass the strawberry mixture through a fine sieve into a jug – don't press down on the fruit or the soup will be cloudy. Discard the solids.

Return the strawberry soup to the saucepan and place over low heat. Dissolve the arrowroot in 1 tablespoon water, then add to the saucepan and gently warm, stirring, until slightly thickened. Remove from the heat and cool. Cover and refrigerate until ready to serve.

To serve, divide the strawberry soup among shallow serving dishes. Place a scoop of sorbet in the centre and garnish with raspberries. **Serves 4-6**

* Arrowroot and goat's milk are available from supermarkets.

Poached pears with chocolate mousse and pistachio soil

4 pears (such as
    beurre bosc)
1 lemon, halved
400g caster sugar
1⅓ cups (330ml) verjuice*
1 vanilla bean, split,
    seeds scraped

Chocolate mousse
¼ cup (55g) caster sugar
1 tsp instant coffee
2 tbs brandy
200g dark chocolate, finely
    chopped, plus extra melted
    dark chocolate to serve
3 eggwhites
¾ cup (185ml) thickened
    cream, plus extra whipped
    cream to serve (optional)

Pistachio soil
25g caster sugar
10g almond meal
20g pistachio kernels
¼ cup (35g) plain flour
20g unsalted butter, melted

For the chocolate mousse, place the sugar, coffee, brandy and ½ cup (125ml) water in a saucepan over medium-high heat and bring to the boil, stirring to dissolve the sugar and coffee. Place the finely chopped chocolate in a blender, then, with the motor running, carefully pour in the hot coffee mixture through the feeder tube, blending until the chocolate has melted. Add the eggwhites and cream to the blender and pulse until just combined. Transfer the mousse to a bowl, cover and refrigerate for at least 4 hours or overnight.

Meanwhile, preheat the oven to 120°C. Line a baking tray with baking paper.

For the pistachio soil, place the sugar, almond meal, pistachios and flour in a mini food processor and whiz until the mixture resembles fine crumbs. Stir through the melted butter, then spread out onto the lined baking tray. Bake for 1 hour, stirring once, or until the crumbs are dry and lightly golden. Cool.

Peel, halve and core the pears, leaving the stalks intact. Rub the flesh with the lemon. Place the sugar and verjuice in a saucepan with the vanilla pod and seeds. Stir over a low heat to dissolve the sugar, then add the pears. If the liquid doesn't quite cover the pears, add enough water to cover. Cover the surface closely with a piece of baking paper cut to fit, then cook the pears for 20-25 minutes until tender and just translucent (the time will vary depending on the ripeness of the pears). Cool the pears in the syrup, then refrigerate until ready to serve.

Place 2 pear halves on each serving plate, add a scoop of chocolate mousse, drizzle with the melted chocolate, sprinkle with the pistachio soil and serve with whipped cream, if desired. **Serves 4**

* Verjuice is unripe grape juice, available from delis and gourmet food shops.

Little black dress chocolate cake

Every girl should have a little black dress in her wardrobe – one of those outfits you can bring out and wow everyone with confidence. This cake is just that: simple, rich, and very sexy. Keep it plain or accessorise with silver or gold jewellery. But small portions, please, or you won't fit into the other little black dress.

500g good-quality dark chocolate, chopped

125g unsalted butter, chopped

6 eggs, separated

90g caster sugar

150ml thickened cream

2 tbs dark rum or brandy

1 tsp vanilla extract

½ tsp cream of tartar

4 cups chocolate ganache (see 'Basics', p 296)

Edible silver or gold leaf*, to serve

Preheat the oven to 180°C. Grease a 24cm springform cake pan and line the base with baking paper.

Place the chocolate and butter in a bowl set over a saucepan of gently simmering water (don't let the bowl touch the water). Stir until the mixture is smooth and combined, then remove the bowl from the heat and set aside to cool slightly.

Place the egg yolks and sugar in an electric mixer and beat until thick and pale. Stir in the cream, rum, vanilla and cooled chocolate mixture.

Whisk the eggwhites and cream of tartar in a clean, dry bowl until soft peaks form. In 3 batches, gently fold the eggwhite into the chocolate mixture with a metal spoon, trying to keep as much air in the mixture as possible. Spread into the prepared pan and bake for 25 minutes until a skewer inserted into the centre comes out with a few moist crumbs. Cool completely in the pan on a wire rack.

Run a knife around the edge of the cake to remove from the pan. Spread the ganache over the cooled cake and garnish with silver or gold leaf. **Serves 8-10**

* Edible silver and gold leaf are available from cake decorating shops and stationery shops.

East meets West

I don't like the term 'fusion food', but I love experimenting with Asian flavours. It's fun to take traditional recipes such as burgers, caesar salad and creme caramels and give them an exotic twist using ingredients from the East.

Spicy fishcakes with pickled-ginger mayonnaise

300g hot-smoked salmon*
  or trout*
2 cups (about 400g) mashed
  potato, cooled completely
4 spring onions, thinly sliced
1 tbs green Thai curry paste
1 small red chilli, seeds
  removed, finely chopped
2 tbs finely chopped
  coriander
1 egg, lightly beaten
½ cup (75g) plain flour
Sunflower oil, to shallow-fry
Pickled ginger and
  lemon wedges, to serve

Pickled-ginger mayonnaise
½ cup (150g) mayonnaise
  (preferably Japanese*)
2 tbs chopped pickled
  ginger, plus 1 tbs
  pickling juice

Remove the skin and any bones from the fish and flake into small pieces. Place the fish in a bowl with the potato, spring onion, curry paste, chilli, coriander and egg. Season well and then mix with a fork until combined. Divide the mixture into 6 portions, then use damp hands to mould into patties. Chill for 30 minutes or until firm.

Meanwhile, for the pickled ginger mayonnaise, combine the mayonnaise, pickled ginger and pickling juice in a bowl. Cover and keep chilled until ready to serve.

Place the flour in a shallow bowl and season. Coat the fishcakes in the flour, shaking off any excess. Heat 3cm oil in a large frypan over medium heat. Fry the fishcakes for 2 minutes each side or until golden and crisp.

Season the fishcakes and serve with the pickled-ginger mayonnaise, pickled ginger and lemon wedges. **Makes 6**

* Hot-smoked salmon, hot-smoked trout and Japanese mayonnaise are available from supermarkets and gourmet food shops.

Duck wonton soup

150g dried shiitake
  mushrooms*
½ Chinese roast duck*
½ bunch coriander,
  leaves picked, stems
  and roots reserved
3cm piece ginger, peeled
2 tbs light soy sauce
8 spring onions, trimmed
2 tbs oyster sauce
32 wonton wrappers*
2 baby bok choy, halved
1 long red chilli, thinly sliced

Soak the shiitake mushrooms in 1 cup (250ml) boiling water for 15 minutes. Drain the mushrooms, then finely chop the caps, reserving the stalks, and set aside.

Finely chop the duck meat, reserving the bones, and set aside. Roughly chop the coriander stems and roots, then set aside.

Place the mushroom stalks, duck bones, coriander stems and roots, ginger, soy sauce and 4 spring onions in a saucepan with 1.5L cold water and bring to the boil. Reduce the heat to low and simmer for 1 hour, skimming the surface occasionally. Strain through a sieve into a clean saucepan, discarding the solids.

Meanwhile, finely chop the remaining 4 spring onions and most of the coriander leaves and place in a bowl with the duck meat, chopped mushroom and oyster sauce, then mix to combine. Arrange the wonton wrappers on a clean work surface and place 1 teaspoon duck mixture in the centre of each. Brush the edges with cold water and lift the corners up to meet in the centre, then pinch to seal. Cover wontons with a damp tea towel and refrigerate until ready to serve.

Return the stock to medium-high heat. Add the bok choy and cook for 2-3 minutes until tender. Keep warm.

In batches, cook the wontons in boiling salted water for 1-2 minutes until they float to the surface. Remove with a slotted spoon and add to the soup. Ladle the soup into bowls, garnish with chilli and remaining coriander leaves and serve. **Serves 4-6**

✱ Dried shiitake mushrooms and wonton wrappers are available from Asian food shops. Chinese roast duck is from Chinese takeaway shops.

Chinese pork buns

These flavoursome Asian buns are a hit at cocktail parties. They're inspired by a dish at Ms. G's, a modern Asian restaurant in Sydney.

2 tbs rice vinegar

2 tbs caster sugar

1 carrot, cut into matchsticks

2 Lebanese cucumbers, seeds removed, cut into matchsticks

¼ cup (60ml) Sriracha Chilli Sauce*

¼ cup (60ml) mayonnaise (preferably Japanese*)

20 small (7cm) white bread rolls*, split

300g good-quality chicken liver pâté

600g Chinese roast pork belly*, sliced

1 cup coriander leaves

1 cup micro cress*

Combine vinegar, sugar and 1 teaspoon salt in a bowl. Stir to dissolve the sugar. Add the carrot and cucumber and stand for at least 10 minutes. Drain well and set aside.

Combine the chilli sauce and mayonnaise in a bowl and set aside.

Lightly toast the buns, then spread the base of each with a generous amount of pâté. Fill the buns with slices of pork belly and top with a little pickled carrot and cucumber, coriander and micro cress. Drizzle with the chilli mayonnaise and serve. **Makes 20**

* Sriracha Chilli Sauce is available from Asian food shops. Japanese mayonnaise is available from supermarkets. Small bread rolls are available from selected bakeries. Chinese roast pork belly is available from Chinese takeaway shops. Micro cress is available from farmers' markets and selected greengrocers.

Salt & pepper quail with chilli sauce

⅓ cup (50g) cornflour
2½ tbs ground Szechaun
   peppercorns*
1 tbs dried chilli flakes
6 quail legs* and
   6 quail breasts*
Sunflower oil, to deep-fry
Sweet chilli sauce and lime
   wedges, to serve

Seasoned salt

1 tsp sea salt
1 tsp ground Szechaun
   peppercorns*
1 tsp dried chilli flakes

Preheat the oven to 170°C. Line a baking tray with baking paper.

Combine the cornflour, Szechaun peppercorns and chilli flakes in a bowl with 1 tablespoon ground black pepper. Pat the quail pieces dry with paper towel, then toss in the flour mixture to coat, shaking off any excess. Set aside.

For the seasoned salt, combine all ingredients in a bowl and set aside.

Half-fill a deep-fryer or large saucepan with oil and heat to 190°C (a cube of bread will turn golden in 30 seconds).

In batches, deep-fry the quail for 2-3 minutes until golden and crisp. Remove with a slotted spoon and drain on paper towel. Transfer the quail to the lined tray and bake for 5 minutes until cooked through.

Sprinkle the seasoned salt over the quail, then serve with sweet chilli sauce and lime wedges. **Serves 4**

* Ground Szechaun peppercorns are available from Asian food shops and Herbie's Spices (herbies.com.au). Quail legs and breasts are available from poultry shops and Game Farm (gamefarm.com.au).

Bacon & egg fried rice

¼ cup (60ml) sunflower oil
12 green prawns, peeled,
    deveined, chopped
1 tbs finely grated
    lemongrass stem
    (inner core only)
6 shiitake mushrooms, sliced
4 rashers bacon, rind
    removed, finely chopped
2 garlic cloves,
    finely chopped
2 tbs grated ginger
1 small red chilli, seeds
    removed, finely chopped
1 cup (120g) frozen peas,
    blanched, refreshed
4 cups cooked jasmine rice
5 spring onions, thinly sliced
    on the diagonal
¼ cup (60ml) light soy sauce,
    plus extra to serve
4 quail eggs*
Chilli sauce, to serve

Heat 1 tablespoon sunflower oil in a wok over medium-high heat. Season the prawns, then add to the wok and stir-fry until almost cooked through. Remove the prawns from the wok and set aside.

Add 1 tablespoon oil to the wok. Add the lemongrass, mushroom, bacon, garlic, ginger and chilli, then stir-fry for 2-3 minutes until fragrant and the bacon is crispy. Return the prawns to the wok with the peas and rice, then stir-fry until warmed through. Add the spring onion and soy sauce, toss to combine, then keep warm and set aside.

Add remaining 1 tablespoon oil to a clean, non-stick frypan over medium-high heat. Break the eggs into the pan and fry for 1-2 minutes until the eggwhites are opaque.

Divide the fried rice among 4 serving bowls and place a fried quail egg on top. Serve with a dash of chilli sauce and extra soy sauce. **Serves 4**

＊ Quail eggs are from Asian food shops and selected poultry shops.

Salty, spicy, sour and sweet are
the main elements in the
flavours of the East.

Angel hair pasta with larb

¼ cup (60ml) sunflower oil
150g mixed Asian
    mushrooms* (such as
    shiitake, shimeji and
    enoki), whole or sliced
1 tbs sesame oil
2 long red chillies, seeds
    removed, finely chopped
3cm piece ginger, grated
4 kaffir lime leaves*,
    inner stem removed,
    very finely shredded
500g chicken mince
2 tbs fish sauce
2 tbs light soy sauce
1 cup coriander leaves
2 cups Thai basil leaves*
Juice of 1 lime, plus lime
    halves to serve
500g angel hair pasta

Heat 2 tablespoons sunflower oil in a wok over high heat. Add the mushrooms and stir-fry for 1-2 minutes until starting to wilt. Remove from wok and set aside.

Add 2 teaspoons sesame oil and remaining 1 tablespoon oil to the wok, then add the chilli, ginger and kaffir lime leaves, and stir-fry for 30 seconds or until fragrant. Add the chicken and stir-fry for a further 3-4 minutes until browned all over. Return the mushrooms to the wok with the fish sauce, soy sauce, coriander and 1 cup Thai basil, then reduce heat to low and cook until warmed through. Stir through the lime juice. Keep warm and set aside.

Meanwhile, cook the pasta according to the packet instructions. Drain, reserving ⅓ cup (80ml) cooking water. Return the pasta to the pan and toss with the reserved water and remaining 2 teaspoons sesame oil.

Divide pasta among bowls, top with the larb, then garnish with remaining 1 cup Thai basil and serve with lime halves. **Serves 4**

* Asian mushrooms, kaffir lime leaves and Thai basil are available from Asian food shops and selected greengrocers.

Soba noodles with hot-smoked salmon and soy dressing

½ cup (125ml) rice vinegar
2 tbs finely grated ginger
1½ tbs soy sauce
2 garlic cloves, crushed
1 tsp sesame oil
¼ cup (60ml) sunflower oil
270g soba noodles*
2 cups (300g) frozen
   podded edamame
   (young green soy beans)*
2 x 150g hot-smoked salmon
   portions*, flaked
1 sheet nori seaweed*,
   cut into thin strips
2 spring onions, thinly sliced
   on the diagonal
2 tsp toasted sesame seeds
Micro coriander*, to serve

Combine the vinegar, ginger, soy sauce, garlic and sesame oil in a bowl. Slowly whisk in the sunflower oil and set aside.

Cook the noodles according to the packet instructions, adding the edamame for the final 3 minutes of cooking time. Drain and refresh, then place in a large bowl with the salmon and half the nori strips. Drizzle over the dressing and toss to combine.

Divide the noodle mixture among serving bowls. Garnish with spring onion, sesame seeds, micro coriander and remaining nori strips. **Serves 4**

* Soba noodles, edamame beans, hot-smoked salmon and nori seaweed are available from supermarkets. Micro coriander is available from farmers' markets and selected greengrocers.

Panko-crumbed chicken caesar salad

1 tbs grated ginger

1 tbs light soy sauce

2 tsp oyster sauce

2 tsp tomato sauce (ketchup)

2 tsp sesame oil

2 x 170g skinless chicken
  breast fillets

1 baguette, thinly sliced

¼ cup (50g) rice flour

2 eggs, lightly beaten

2 cups (100g) panko
  breadcrumbs*

Sunflower oil, to deep-fry

2 baby cos lettuce,
  leaves separated

250g punnet cherry
  tomatoes, halved

3 hard-boiled eggs, quartered

Shaved parmesan, to serve

Caesar salad dressing

1 egg

1 garlic clove, finely chopped

1 tsp Dijon mustard

½ tsp Worcestershire sauce

2 anchovy fillets in oil, drained

150ml extra virgin olive oil

Juice of 1 lime

½ cup (40g) grated parmesan

Combine the ginger, soy sauce, oyster sauce, ketchup and sesame oil in a bowl. Cut the chicken into 2cm strips, then add to the soy mixture and toss to coat well. Cover and refrigerate for 2-3 hours.

Meanwhile, for the caesar salad dressing, place the egg, garlic, Dijon, Worcestershire and anchovies in a food processor and whiz to combine. With the motor running, slowly drizzle in the oil until thick and combined. Stir in the lime juice and parmesan, then season. Loosen with a little warm water if too thick. Keep chilled until ready to serve.

Heat a chargrill pan over medium-high heat. Lightly grill the baguette slices for 1-2 minutes each side until crispy. Set aside.

Drain the chicken from the marinade, allowing any excess to drip off. Place rice flour, egg and panko breadcrumbs in 3 separate bowls. Dip chicken first in the flour, then in the egg, then coat in the panko crumbs.

Half-fill a deep-fryer or wok with oil and heat to 190°C (a cube of bread will turn golden in 30 seconds). In batches, fry the chicken for 2-3 minutes until crisp, golden and cooked through. Remove with a slotted spoon and drain on paper towel.

Place the lettuce, tomato, egg, baguette croutons and chicken in a large serving bowl and gently toss to combine. Top the salad with the shaved parmesan, drizzle with the dressing, then season well and serve. **Serves 4-6**

✽ Panko breadcrumbs are from Asian food shops and supermarkets.

Ginger cakes with chilli icing

175g unsalted butter, softened

175g caster sugar

3 eggs

1⅔ cups (250g) self-raising flour, sifted

1 tsp ground ginger

Pinch of cayenne pepper

100g preserved ginger in syrup*, finely chopped, plus extra ⅓ cup (80ml) syrup

1 long red chilli, seeds removed, finely chopped

1 cup (150g) icing sugar, sifted

Preheat the oven to 180°C. Grease a 12-hole muffin pan.

Beat the butter and sugar in an electric mixer until thick and pale. Add the eggs, one at a time, beating well after each addition. Fold in the flour and spices, then stir in most of the chopped ginger and 2 tablespoons extra syrup. Spoon into the muffin holes and bake for 20 minutes or until golden and a skewer inserted into the centre comes out clean. Cool slightly in the pan, then invert onto a wire rack and cool completely.

Meanwhile, soak the chilli in 1 tablespoon boiling water for 15 minutes. Combine the chilli and soaking liquid with the remaining 2 tablespoons ginger syrup. Add icing sugar and stir until a soft icing.

Drizzle the chilli icing over the cooled cakes, then garnish with the remaining chopped ginger. **Makes 12**

* Preserved ginger in syrup is available from Asian food shops and selected supermarkets.

Pineapple caramels

It's amazing how luscious these pineapple caramels are – with not a drop of cream.

1 cup (220g) caster sugar
4 eggs, plus 4 extra
   egg yolks
2 cups (500ml) unsweetened
   pineapple juice
Dried pineapple slices*,
   to serve

Preheat the oven to 160°C. Grease four 1 cup (250ml) dariole moulds or ramekins.

Place ½ cup (110g) sugar and 2 tablespoons water in a saucepan over low heat, stirring until the sugar has dissolved. Increase the heat to medium and cook, swirling the pan occasionally, for 4-5 minutes until a golden caramel. Carefully pour into the base of the moulds.

Beat the eggs and extra yolks with the remaining ½ cup (110g) sugar until just combined. Stir in the pineapple juice and divide among the moulds. Place the moulds in a baking dish and pour enough boiling water into the dish to come halfway up the sides of the moulds. Bake for 40 minutes until the pineapple caramels are firm and just set, but still have a slight wobble in the centre. Remove the moulds from the pan and cool, then refrigerate for at least 4 hours.

To serve, dip the base of each mould in boiling water for a few seconds and run a knife around the edge. Invert each pineapple caramel on to a plate and serve with dried pineapple. **Makes 4**

* Dried pineapple slices are available from health food shops and Whisk & Pin (whiskandpin.com.au).

Beyond wicked

Wicked has been one of the most popular features in *delicious.* over the past 10 years, but now we're taking it to the next level. Think rich, over-the-top and impressive desserts, cakes and pastries. They're not for the fainthearted – but then again, if they were, they wouldn't be beyond wicked!

Chocolate-swirl meringues with glazed strawberries

4 eggwhites
1 cup (220g) caster sugar
2 tsp cornflour
1 tsp white wine vinegar
1 tbs cocoa
⅓ cup (110g) good-quality
   strawberry jam
250g punnet strawberries,
   hulled, halved
300ml thickened cream
2 tbs icing sugar, sifted
1 vanilla bean, split,
   seeds scraped

Preheat the oven to 140°C. Line a large baking tray with baking paper.

Place the eggwhites and caster sugar in a heatproof bowl set over a saucepan of barely simmering water (don't let the bowl touch the water), stirring until the sugar has dissolved. Transfer the mixture to an electric mixer and whisk until firm peaks form. Carefully fold in the cornflour and vinegar with a metal spoon until just combined. Sift the cocoa over the eggwhite mixture and carefully stir through with the metal spoon until you have lovely chocolate swirls.

Spoon the mixture into 6 large rounds on the prepared tray, making a slight indent in the centre of each with the back of the spoon. Place in the oven and immediately reduce the temperature to 120°C. Bake for 1¼ hours or until crisp and dry. Switch the oven off and leave the door slightly ajar. Allow the meringues to cool completely in the oven.

Meanwhile, place the jam and ¼ cup (60ml) cold water in a saucepan over low heat and stir gently until the jam is melted and syrupy. Remove from heat, then stir through the strawberries. Allow to cool.

Whisk the cream with the icing sugar and vanilla seeds until soft peaks form. Keep chilled until ready to serve.

To serve, top the meringues with the whipped cream and spoon over glazed strawberries and a little syrup. **Serves 6**

Blueberry, mango & praline trifle

200g liquid glucose*
500g caster sugar
200g slivered almonds
2 tbs lemon juice
1 cup (250ml) dry Marsala
  (Sicilian fortified wine)
500g blueberries
5 eggs, separated
1 vanilla bean, split,
  seeds scraped
500g mascarpone
1 large pandoro*
  or 1 store-bought
  sponge cake, cut
  into 2cm-thick slices
2 mangoes, sliced

Place the liquid glucose and 250g caster sugar in a saucepan over low heat, stirring until sugar has dissolved. Increase heat to medium-high and cook, swirling the pan occasionally, for 5-6 minutes until a golden caramel. Add the almonds, then pour the caramel onto a lightly greased baking tray. Allow to cool, then break the praline into rough shards. Reserve a few shards to garnish, then place the remaining praline in a food processor and pulse until a fine powder. Set aside.

Meanwhile, place lemon juice, 125g caster sugar and ½ cup (125ml) Marsala in a saucepan over medium heat, stirring until the sugar has dissolved. Add the blueberries, then reduce heat to low and simmer for 5 minutes or until slightly reduced. Allow to cool.

Place the egg yolks and remaining 125g caster sugar in a bowl and beat until thick and pale. Add the vanilla seeds and mascarpone and beat until smooth. In a clean, separate bowl, whisk the eggwhites until soft peaks form, then fold into the mascarpone mixture.

Place a layer of pandoro or sponge slices in a 1.5L glass serving dish and drizzle with about 2 tbs Marsala, then spread with one-third of the mascarpone mixture. Top with one-third of the mango and drizzle with one-third of the blueberries and their syrup. Sprinkle with half the crushed praline. Repeat the layers. Top with a final layer of cake. Drizzle with the remaining Marsala, then top with the remaining mango and mascarpone mixture. Cover with plastic wrap and refrigerate for at least 2 hours to allow flavours to develop.

Drizzle over the remaining blueberries and their syrup, then garnish with praline shards and serve. **Serves 8-10**

* Liquid glucose is available from supermarkets. Pandoro is an Italian yeast-based cake available from Italian and gourmet food shops.

Millionaire's eclairs

Filled with rich, gooey dulce de leche and decorated with flecks of gold, these glittering eclairs are pure opulence.

100g unsalted butter

1⅓ cups (200g) plain flour, sifted

5 eggs

600ml thickened cream

170g dark chocolate, chopped

¼ cup (90g) liquid glucose*

1 vanilla bean, split, seeds scraped

2 tbs icing sugar, sifted

450g dulce de leche*

Edible gold leaf*, to serve

Preheat the oven to 220°C. Line 2 large baking trays with baking paper.

Place the butter in a saucepan with 1¼ cups (310ml) water over medium-high heat. Bring to the boil, then remove from the heat. Add the flour and beat well with a wooden spoon until smooth. Return the pan to low heat and continue to cook, stirring, until the mixture comes away from the sides of the pan. Transfer to an electric mixer, then add the eggs, one at a time, beating well after each addition.

Spoon the choux pastry into a piping bag fitted with a 1cm plain nozzle. Pipe 12cm lengths onto the baking trays, leaving about 3cm between each one, to make 24 eclairs. Bake for 15 minutes, then reduce heat to 180°C and bake for a further 15 minutes or until crisp and golden. Switch the oven off and leave the door slightly ajar. Allow the eclairs to cool completely in the oven.

Meanwhile, place ½ cup (125ml) cream in a saucepan and bring to just below boiling point. Remove from heat, then add the chocolate and glucose and stir until melted and glossy. Set aside to cool slightly.

Whisk the remaining cream with the vanilla seeds, icing sugar and dulce de leche until stiff peaks form. Keep chilled until ready to use.

To assemble, use a serrated knife to cut each eclair in half lengthways. Dip the tops in the chocolate glaze and place on a wire rack to set. Pipe or spoon the dulce de leche filling into the eclairs, then replace the tops and garnish with gold leaf. **Makes 24**

* Liquid glucose is available from supermarkets. Dulce de leche is available from gourmet food shops and delis. Edible gold leaf is available from cake decorating shops and stationery shops.

Black-bottom lemon meringue ice cream pie

2 eggs, separated,
    plus 2 extra eggwhites
1 cup (220g) caster sugar
100g unsalted butter,
    softened
Finely grated zest
    of 2 lemons, plus
    2 tbs lemon juice
300g packet dark chocolate
    shortcrust pastry*
1L good-quality
    vanilla bean ice cream
Pinch of cream of tartar

You'll need a kitchen blowtorch for this recipe.

Place the egg yolks and ½ cup (110g) sugar in a heatproof bowl set over a pan of simmering water (don't let the bowl touch the water). Whisk until well combined. Add the butter and lemon zest and juice, then cook, whisking occasionally, for 10-15 minutes until thick and smooth. Cover the surface closely with a piece of baking paper, set aside to cool, then chill for 30 minutes or until set.

Meanwhile, grease a 24cm-wide, 4cm-deep loose-bottomed tart pan. Roll out the pastry on a lightly floured work surface until large enough to fit the tart pan. Line the pan with the pastry, then chill for 15 minutes.

Preheat the oven to 180°C.

Line the pastry case with baking paper and fill with baking weights or uncooked rice. Bake for 10 minutes, then remove paper and weights and bake for a further 5 minutes until pastry is crisp and dry. Cool.

Allow the ice cream to soften at room temperature for 20 minutes, then spread half the ice cream into the tart shell and dollop with half the lemon curd, then swirl the lemon curd through the ice cream using a skewer. Repeat with remaining ice cream and lemon curd, then return to the freezer for 3 hours or until firm.

Using electric beaters, whisk the 4 eggwhites with cream of tartar until soft peaks form. Gradually add the remaining ½ cup (110g) sugar, 1 tablespoon at a time, and continue to whisk until firm peaks form. Dollop the meringue mixture over the pie, completely covering the ice cream and swirling with the back of a spoon to create little peaks and folds. Return to the freezer for at least 2 hours.

Just before serving, use a kitchen blowtorch to caramelise the edges of the meringue. Cut into slices and serve immediately. **Serves 6-8**

* We used Careme dark chocolate shortcrust pastry. For stockists, visit: caremepastry.com.

Chocolate mousse tarts

300g packet dark chocolate
   shortcrust pastry*
125g good-quality dark
   chocolate, chopped,
   plus extra 25g melted
   dark chocolate to brush
250g Nutella or other
   hazelnut spread
450ml milk
300ml pure (thin) cream
3 eggs
Chocolate shavings
   and icing sugar, to serve

Preheat the oven to 170°C.

Use the pastry to line six 10cm-wide, 3cm-deep loose-bottomed tart pans, then chill for 15 minutes.

Line the pastry cases with baking paper and baking weights or uncooked rice. Bake for 10 minutes, then remove paper and weights and bake for a further 3 minutes until the pastry is crisp and dry. Cool slightly, then brush the inside of the cases with a little melted chocolate to form a seal. Set aside.

Reduce the oven temperature to 160°C.

Meanwhile, place Nutella and chopped chocolate in a bowl and set aside. Place the milk and cream in a saucepan and bring to just below boiling point. Pour the cream mixture over the chocolate and Nutella and stir until melted and smooth. Add the eggs, one at a time, beating well with a wooden spoon until well combined.

Pour the chocolate mousse into the tart shells. Bake for 10-15 minutes until almost set. Remove from the oven and cool completely.

Scatter the chocolate shavings over the tarts, dust with icing sugar and serve. **Makes 6**

* We used Careme dark chocolate shortcrust pastry. For stockists, visit: caremepastry.com.

Don't say you
won't be tempted
– these desserts are
irresistibly good.

Gin & tonic tart

4 eggs
¾ cup (165g) caster sugar
1 tbs finely grated lemon
    zest, plus ¾ cup (185ml)
    strained lemon juice
150ml thickened cream
¼ cup (60ml) gin

Pastry
200g plain flour, sifted
¼ cup (35g) icing sugar,
    sifted
75g chilled unsalted
    butter, chopped
2 tsp lemon zest
1 egg yolk
¼ cup (60ml) chilled
    tonic water

Gin & tonic syrup
150g caster sugar
1 cup (250ml) tonic water
Very thinly pared zest
    and juice of 2 lemons
¼ cup (60ml) gin
5 juniper berries*,
    lightly bruised

For the pastry, place the flour, icing sugar, butter and lemon zest in a food processor and whiz until mixture resembles fine crumbs. Add the yolk and tonic water and process until the mixture comes together in a smooth ball. Enclose in plastic wrap and chill for 30 minutes.

Preheat the oven to 180°C. Grease a 23cm loose-bottomed tart pan.

Roll out the pastry on a lightly floured surface until 5mm thick, then use it to line the tart pan. Chill for a further 15 minutes.

Line the pastry case with baking paper and fill with baking weights or uncooked rice. Bake for 10 minutes, then remove the paper and weights and bake for a further 5 minutes or until the pastry is golden and dry. Allow to cool.

Whisk the eggs, caster sugar, lemon zest and juice, cream and gin together until combined. Pour the filling into the tart shell and bake for 20-25 minutes until just set.

Meanwhile, for the syrup, place the sugar, tonic water and lemon juice in a saucepan over low heat, stirring to dissolve the sugar. Add the gin and juniper berries and simmer for 5-10 minutes until slightly thickened. Blanch the lemon zest in boiling water for 2 minutes, drain, then add to the syrup. Simmer for a further 5 minutes, then cool.

Remove the juniper berries from the gin and tonic syrup, then drizzle over the tart and serve. **Serves 8-10**

✳ Juniper berries are available from supermarkets and delis.

Turkish delight cheesecake

300g shortbread
  or digestive biscuits
¼ cup (25g) cocoa, sifted
80g unsalted butter, melted
8 gold-strength
  gelatine leaves*
1kg cream cheese,
  at room temperature
1¼ cups (275g) caster sugar
⅓ cup (80ml) milk
300ml thickened cream
¼ cup (60ml) rosewater
2 x 250g punnets
  strawberries,
  hulled, halved

Grease a 22cm springform cake pan.

Place the biscuits and cocoa in a food processor and whiz until fine crumbs. Add the butter and pulse to combine. Press mixture into the base of the cake pan, then chill while you make the filling.

Soak 5 gelatine leaves in cold water for 5 minutes.

Meanwhile, place cream cheese and ¾ cup (165g) sugar in cleaned food processor and whiz until smooth. Place the milk in a saucepan over medium-high heat and bring to just below boiling point. Squeeze excess water from the gelatine, then add the gelatine to the milk, stirring until the gelatine has dissolved. Cool slightly, then add to the cream cheese mixture in the food processor and whiz to combine. Transfer to a bowl.

Beat the cream with electric beaters until soft peaks form, then fold into the cream cheese mixture with 1 tablespoon rosewater. Pour the filling over the biscuit base and gently tap the pan on the bench to dispel any air pockets. Cover in plastic wrap and chill for 4 hours or until filling is set.

Meanwhile, place the strawberries and remaining ½ cup (110g) sugar in a large bowl with ½ cup (125ml) water, stirring to dissolve the sugar. Cover the bowl tightly with foil and place over a pan of simmering water (don't let the bowl touch the water). Simmer for 20 minutes, topping up the pan with more water if needed, until the strawberries are very soft.

Soak remaining 3 gelatine leaves in cold water for 5 minutes.

Pass the strawberry mixture through a fine sieve into a bowl – don't press down on the fruit, or the jelly will be cloudy. While the juice is warm, squeeze excess water from the gelatine, then stir the gelatine into the juice until dissolved. Stir in remaining 2 tablespoons rosewater. Cool completely, then place in the fridge for 15 minutes until just starting to thicken. Pour the strawberry jelly over the cheesecake, then return to the fridge for 3-4 hours until the top has completely set. **Serves 8-10**

* Gelatine leaves are available from gourmet food shops.

Triple-chocolate fudge cookies

250g unsalted butter
¾ cup (165g) caster sugar
¾ cup (185g) brown sugar
1 tsp vanilla extract
1 egg
2 cups (300g) plain flour,
    sifted
¼ cup (25g) cocoa, sifted
1 tsp bicarbonate of soda
⅓ cup (40g) chopped
    roasted hazelnuts
100g salted caramel
    chocolate*, chopped
150g dark chocolate,
    chopped
150g white chocolate,
    chopped

Preheat the oven to 180°C. Line 2 large baking trays with baking paper.

Place the butter, caster sugar, brown sugar and vanilla extract in an electric mixer and beat until thick and pale. Add the egg and beat until well combined. Sift in flour, cocoa and bicarbonate of soda, then stir in hazelnuts, salted caramel chocolate and ⅔ cup (120g) each of the dark and white chocolate. Roll level tablespoons of cookie dough into balls, then arrange on the trays 5cm apart. Slightly flatten each ball with your hand, then bake for 12 minutes or until just dry on the surface. Allow to cool until slightly firm, then transfer to a wire rack to cool completely.

Place the reserved 30g dark chocolate in a heatproof bowl set over a saucepan of simmering water (don't let the bowl touch the water). Stir until melted, then drizzle over the biscuits. Repeat with the remaining 30g white chocolate. Cool until chocolate sets. **Makes 36 large cookies**

* We used Mazet milk salted caramel chocolate, available from Simon Johnson (simonjohnson.com.au); substitute regular milk chocolate.

Ice cream terrine

This terrine takes a bit of time to assemble as you need to freeze each layer separately, but it's great to have on standby in the freezer for an impressive dessert. Feel free to vary the ice cream flavours with whatever takes your fancy, but try to use good-quality ice cream as it will make such a difference to the end result.

500ml good-quality
   pistachio ice cream
450g Madeira cake, cut
   into thirds lengthways
⅓ cup (80ml) grappa
   (optional)
500ml good-quality
   strawberry ice cream
1L good-quality
   vanilla bean ice cream
½ cup (160g) strawberry jam
250g punnet strawberries,
   hulled, sliced

Line a 2L terrine pan with plastic wrap, leaving plenty of plastic wrap overhanging the sides. Allow the pistachio ice cream to soften at room temperature for 15 minutes.

Cover the terrine base with 1 Maderia slice. Drizzle with one-third of the grappa, then spread over the pistachio ice cream using a palette knife to level the top. Chill in the freezer for 1 hour.

Meanwhile, allow the strawberry ice cream to soften at room temperature for 15 minutes.

Cover the pistachio ice cream with another Madeira slice. Drizzle with another third of the grappa, then spread over strawberry ice cream using a palette knife to level the top. Chill in the freezer for a further 1 hour.

Meanwhile, allow the vanilla bean ice cream to soften at room temperature for 15 minutes or until a spreadable consistency.

Cover the strawberry ice cream with the remaining Madeira slice. Drizzle with the remaining grappa, then carefully turn out the terrine. Use a palette knife to spread the vanilla bean ice cream over all sides of the terrine (if it's a warm day, you may need to pop the terrine back into the freezer a couple of times just to keep it firm). Place the terrine on a baking paper-lined baking tray, cover with plastic wrap and return to the freezer for 4 hours or overnight until completely firm.

Place the strawberry jam in a small saucepan over low heat with ½ cup (125ml) water. Cook, stirring, until smooth. Remove from the heat, then add the strawberries and set aside to cool.

Cut the terrine into thick slices and serve with berries. **Serves 8-10**

Chocolate butterscotch layer cake

2 tbs redcurrant jelly

1 cup (250ml) milk

2½ cups (375g) self-raising flour

1 cup (100g) good-quality cocoa

1 cup (220g) caster sugar

1 firmly packed cup (250g) brown sugar

125g unsalted butter, melted, cooled slightly

1 tsp vanilla extract

6 eggs, lightly beaten

2 cups chocolate ganache (see 'Basics', p 296)

Toffee hazelnuts

1 cup (220g) caster sugar

⅓ cup (80ml) liquid glucose*

15 hazelnuts

Butterscotch cream

600ml thickened cream

3 tbs golden syrup

2 tbs brown sugar

½ tsp vanilla extract

Preheat oven to 160°C. Grease and line two 20cm springform cake pans.

Stir redcurrant jelly with 1 tablespoon milk until smooth. Set aside.

Sift the flour and cocoa into a bowl, then add the caster sugar, brown sugar and ½ teaspoon salt. Add the butter, vanilla, eggs, redcurrant jelly mixture and remaining milk and stir to combine. Divide between the prepared pans, then bake for 45-55 minutes until a skewer inserted into the centre comes out clean. Cool cakes in the pans for 10 minutes, then transfer to a wire rack to cool completely.

Meanwhile, for the toffee hazelnuts, place sugar, glucose and ½ cup (125ml) water in a pan over medium heat, stirring to dissolve sugar. Cook for 6-8 minutes, swirling the pan occasionally, until a golden caramel. Set aside and cool until slightly thickened. Carefully pierce each hazelnut with the tip of a wooden skewer, being careful not to split the nut. Bend the other end of each skewer at a right angle, 3cm in from the end. Place a large sheet of baking paper on the bench. Stack 2 tall saucepans on the paper and place a large baking tray on top of the pans. (The stacked saucepans need to be at least 5cm taller than the skewers.) Dip each hazelnut in the caramel, then hang the bent end of the skewer over the edge of the tray. The caramel will drip down to the paper to form a trail. Cool, then remove the nuts from the skewers.

For the butterscotch cream, place the cream, golden syrup, sugar and vanilla in an electric mixer and beat until stiff peaks form. Keep refrigerated until ready to use.

To assemble, use a serrated knife to halve each cake horizontally to give 4 layers. Place 1 layer on a serving plate, then using a spatula, spread one-third of the butterscotch cream on the cake. Repeat 2 more times, then top with the final layer of cake. Spread the ganache over the top of the cake and decorate with the toffee hazelnuts. **Serves 8-10**

* Liquid glucose is available from supermarkets.

Trattoria at home

A trattoria is a casual, often family-run, eatery serving robust Italian food with a warm generosity of spirit. This isn't the refined cuisine you'd find in the award-winning restaurants of Milan, it's comfort food at its best – simply prepared and without fuss, using fresh, seasonal ingredients.

Scarlatini

The Italians know a thing or two about *aperitivi*. This sparkling strawberry drink with a dash of Frangelico will definitely get the party started.

250g punnet strawberries, hulled, quartered, plus extra to serve
¼ cup (55g) caster sugar
1 tbs lemon juice
¼ cup (60ml) Frangelico or other hazelnut liqueur
750ml chilled prosecco or other sparkling wine

Combine the strawberries, sugar and lemon juice in a heatproof bowl. Cover with foil and place over a saucepan of barely simmering water. Simmer, topping up the saucepan with more water as needed, for 1 hour or until strawberries are very soft.

Pass the strawberry mixture through a fine sieve into a jug – don't press down on the fruit or the liquid will be cloudy. Discard the solids.

Stir the Frangelico into the strawberry mixture, then chill.

To serve, divide the strawberry mixture among 6 serving glasses and top with prosecco or sparkling wine. **Makes 6**

Cheese & fig tarts

3 sheets frozen shortcrust
    pastry, thawed
150g soft goat's cheese
1 cup (240g) ricotta
¼ cup (20g) grated
    parmesan
3 eggs
½ cup (125ml) pure
    (thin) cream
1 tbs rosemary leaves,
    chopped
3 figs, halved
Vincotto* and micro herbs*,
    to serve

Line six 10cm-wide, 3cm-deep loose-bottomed tart pans with the pastry, trimming any excess. Refrigerate for 30 minutes.

Preheat the oven to 180°C.

Prick the pastry with a fork, then line with baking paper and fill with pastry weights or uncooked rice. Bake for 10 minutes, then remove paper and weights. Bake for a further 2 minutes or until the pastry is golden and dry.

Meanwhile, beat goat's cheese, ricotta, parmesan, eggs and cream together, then season. Stir in the rosemary, then divide among the tart cases. Press a fig half, cut-side up, into the filling. Bake for 20-25 minutes until the filling is just set.

Drizzle the tarts with vincotto and garnish with the micro herbs. Serve warm. **Makes 6**

* Vincotto (substitute balsamic glaze) is available from Italian delis and gourmet food shops. Micro herbs are available from farmers' markets and selected greengrocers.

Eggplant pesto timballos

2 garlic cloves,
  finely chopped
½ cup (125ml) extra
  virgin olive oil
2 (about 600g) eggplants,
  cut into 1cm-thick slices
1¼ cups (300g) ricotta
200g jar good-quality pesto
250g punnet vine-ripened
  cherry tomatoes
¼ cup basil leaves

Heat a chargrill pan or barbecue to medium-high heat.

Combine garlic and ⅓ cup (80ml) oil in a bowl. Brush both sides of the eggplant slices with the garlic oil. In batches if necessary, cook the eggplant for 1 minute on one side, then turn at a 90° angle and cook for a further 1 minute – this will create a crisscross pattern on the eggplant slices. Turn the eggplant and repeat the process on the other side. Set aside to cool.

Preheat the oven to 200°C. Grease four 1 cup (250ml) ramekins.

Place ricotta in a bowl and season. Place 1 chargrilled eggplant slice in each ramekin and top each with 1 heaped tablespoon seasoned ricotta, then a tablespoonful of pesto. Repeat the layers with the remaining eggplant, ricotta and pesto, finishing each timballo with an eggplant slice.

Place the ramekins on a baking tray and bake for 15 minutes. Remove the baking tray from the oven and place the tomatoes on the tray with the timballos. Drizzle the tomatoes with 1 tablespoon olive oil, season, then return the tray to the oven for a further 8 minutes or until the tomatoes have just started to soften and the timballos are warmed through. Remove from the oven and rest for 5 minutes.

Heat remaining 1 tablespoon oil in a small frypan over medium heat and carefully cook the basil leaves for 15 seconds or until crispy. Remove the basil from the pan with a slotted spoon and drain on paper towel.

Invert the timballos onto serving plates and season. Garnish with the roasted tomatoes and fried basil leaves and serve. **Serves 4**

Melon, pecorino & prosciutto salad

1 long red chilli,
  seeds removed,
  very finely chopped
½ cup (125ml) extra
  virgin olive oil
¼ cup (60ml) vincotto*
½ honeydew melon
½ rockmelon
12 slices prosciutto, torn
125g shaved pecorino
  pepato*
Mint leaves, to serve

Combine chilli, oil and vincotto in a bowl and season. Set aside.

Cut the melons into thin slices and arrange on serving plates with the prosciutto. Scatter with the pecorino and mint, drizzle with the chilli dressing and serve. **Serves 6**

* Vincotto (substitute balsamic glaze) and pecorino pepato (a hard sheep's milk cheese studded with peppercorns) are available from Italian delis and gourmet food shops.

Farfalle with sausage ragu

This recipe is my family's favourite midweek pasta dish. It's so simple, but packs a punch, especially if you use lovely, spicy Italian sausages.

2 tbs olive oil

100g flat pancetta*, chopped

1 onion, finely chopped

300g good-quality Italian pork sausages, casings removed, chopped

2 x 400g cans chopped tomatoes

½ tsp freshly grated nutmeg

150ml pure (thin) cream

1 tbs finely chopped sage

Juice of ½ lemon

400g farfalle pasta

Chopped flat-leaf parsley, shaved parmesan and crusty bread, to serve

Heat the oil in a large frypan over medium heat. Add the pancetta and onion, then cook, stirring, for 5-6 minutes until the onion is very soft and the pancetta is golden. Add the sausage meat and cook, breaking up any lumps with a wooden spoon, for a further 5-6 minutes until evenly browned. Cool slightly, then transfer to a food processor and pulse several times until all the sausage meat is an even texture.

Return sausage mixture to the pan and place over medium-high heat. Add the tomato and nutmeg to the pan, bring to a simmer, then reduce heat to medium-low and simmer, stirring occasionally, for 15 minutes. Stir through the cream and sage, then simmer for a further 5-6 minutes until thickened. Add the lemon juice to the sauce and season well.

Meanwhile, cook pasta in a large saucepan of boiling salted water according to the packet instructions until al dente. Drain, reserving a little cooking water.

Add enough reserved cooking water to the sauce to loosen slightly. Add the pasta to the sauce and toss to coat. Scatter with the parsley and parmesan, and serve with crusty bread. **Serves 4**

* Flat pancetta is available from delis.

Sometimes a bowl of indulgent *Italian food* is all that you need.

Spaghetti with mussels

¼ cup (60ml) extra virgin
  olive oil
1 long red chilli, seeds
  removed, finely chopped
4 garlic cloves,
  finely chopped
1 onion, finely chopped
1 baby fennel, finely chopped
¾ cup (185ml) dry white wine
400g can chopped tomatoes
1kg pot-ready mussels
400g spaghetti
¼ cup chopped flat-leaf
  parsley
1 tbs grated lemon zest, plus
  lemon halves to serve

Heat the oil in a large saucepan over medium heat. Add the chilli, garlic, onion and fennel, then cook, stirring, for 15 minutes or until softened. Add the wine to the pan and bring to a simmer. Stir in the tomato and cook for 3-4 minutes until slightly reduced. Add the mussels, then cover with a lid. Cook, shaking the pan occasionally, for 2 minutes. Remove opened mussels and set aside. Cook for a further 2 minutes, then discard any mussels that remain closed. Return the opened mussels to the pan and season to taste.

Meanwhile, cook the spaghetti in a large saucepan of boiling salted water according to the packet instructions until al dente, then drain.

Add the spaghetti to the sauce and toss to combine. Scatter with the parsley and lemon zest. Serve with lemon halves. **Serves 4-6**

Tomato, mascarpone & rocket pizza

500g strong (baker's) flour*

7g sachet dried instant yeast

1 tsp caster sugar

1 tbs extra virgin olive oil,
plus extra to drizzle

½ cup (125ml) tomato
passata (sugo)*

½ cup (125g) mascarpone

250g bocconcini, sliced

250g punnet vine-ripened
cherry tomatoes

12 slices prosciutto

1 cup (160g) kalamata
olives

2 cups rocket

Sift flour into a bowl and add the yeast, sugar, oil, 1 teaspoon salt and 300ml warm water. Bring the ingredients together and knead by hand (or in an electric mixer with a dough hook) for 5 minutes or until the dough is smooth and elastic.

Place the dough in a clean, oiled bowl, then cover with a clean tea towel and leave to rise in a warm place for 1-1½ hours until doubled in size.

Preheat the oven to 230°C.

Punch down the dough to expel any trapped air, then divide in half and roll out each portion into a 20cm round. Place each base on an oiled pizza tray and spread with the passata.

Dot the pizza bases with mascarpone, scatter with bocconcini and tomatoes, then leave to rise for a further 10 minutes.

Bake for 12 minutes until the bases are cooked through and cheese has melted. Top with prosciutto, olives and rocket, drizzle with extra olive oil and serve immediately. **Makes 2 large pizzas**

* Strong (baker's) flour and tomato passata (sugo) are available from supermarkets.

Pasta genovese

12 slices flat pancetta*

400g maccheroni al ferretto*
or other short pasta

3 (about 400g) large kipfler
potatoes, peeled, cut
into 1cm-thick slices

200g green beans, trimmed

1 cup (120g) frozen peas

Shaved parmesan, to serve

Pesto

2 firmly packed cups
basil leaves

⅓ cup (50g) pine nuts

2 garlic cloves

1¼ cups (100g) grated
parmesan

150ml extra virgin olive oil

Preheat the oven to 200°C. Line a baking tray with baking paper.

Arrange the pancetta in a single layer on the lined tray. Bake for 8-10 minutes until crispy. Cool for 5 minutes, then break into large pieces.

Meanwhile, for the pesto, place the basil, nuts, garlic and parmesan in a food processor and whiz until combined. With the motor running, add the oil in a slow, steady stream until a smooth paste. Set aside. (The pesto will keep in the refrigerator in a jar under a thin layer of olive oil for up to 1 week.)

Cook the pasta in a large saucepan of salted boiling water according to the packet instructions, adding the potato for the final 8 minutes and the beans and peas for the final 1 minute of cooking time, until the pasta is al dente and the vegetables are tender. Drain the pasta and vegetables, reserving the cooking water.

Toss the pasta and vegetables with the pesto, adding enough reserved cooking water so the pesto coats the pasta. Serve the pasta topped with the crispy pancetta and shaved parmesan. **Serves 4**

✱ Flat pancetta and maccheroni al ferretto are available from delis.

Chocolate-chip tiramisu

6 eggs, separated
400g caster sugar
1kg mascarpone
200g dark chocolate
200ml strong espresso
¾ firmly packed cup
  (185g) brown sugar
200ml Kahlua or
  other coffee liqueur
2 tbs cocoa, plus
  extra to dust
36 sponge finger biscuits
  (savoiardi)

Place the egg yolks and 200g caster sugar in a bowl set over a pan of simmering water (don't let the bowl touch the water). Whisk until thick and pale, then remove from heat and set aside to cool.

Gradually beat the mascarpone into the cooled egg yolk mixture until smooth and well combined. Finely chop 150g chocolate and fold into mascarpone mixture. Set aside.

In a clean, dry bowl, whisk the eggwhites until soft peaks form. Gradually add the remaining 200g sugar, whisking until stiff and glossy, then fold into the mascarpone mixture.

Combine espresso, brown sugar, Kahlua and cocoa in a saucepan. Stir over low heat until sugar has dissolved, then remove from the heat and allow to cool.

Dip 12 sponge fingers into the espresso mixture, then arrange in a 20cm square loose-bottomed cake pan or a 1.5L serving dish, cutting the sponge fingers to fit. Spread with one-third of the mascarpone mixture. Repeat the layers twice more, alternating the direction of the sponge fingers – this will help keep the tiramisu stable. Cover and chill for at least 4 hours or overnight.

To serve, shave the remaining 50g chocolate into shards using a vegetable peeler and scatter over the tiramisu. Dust with extra cocoa and cut into slices. **Serves 8-10**

Ricotta & Marsala cheesecake

100g raisins

⅓ cup (80ml) Marsala
(Sicilian fortified wine)

150g amaretti biscuits

150g digestive biscuits

150g unsalted butter,
melted, cooled

500g ricotta

1 cup (250g) mascarpone

150ml thickened cream

5 eggs

1¼ cups (275g) caster sugar

1 tbs plain flour

Finely grated zest
and juice of 1 lemon

Icing sugar, to dust

Preheat the oven to 180°C. Grease and line a 22cm springform cake pan.

Place the raisins and Marsala in a saucepan over medium heat and bring to a simmer. Remove from heat and set aside to cool.

Place the biscuits and butter in a food processor and whiz until fine crumbs. Press into the base of the cake pan and chill for 15 minutes. Bake for 10 minutes until just set and golden. Allow to cool.

Meanwhile, place the ricotta, mascarpone, cream, eggs, sugar, flour and lemon zest and juice in a food processor and whiz until smooth. Strain raisins, reserving the Marsala. Stir the Marsala through the cheese mixture.

Pour the cheese mixture onto the biscuit base, then sprinkle the raisins over the top (the raisins will sink to the bottom as the cake cooks). Bake for 1¼ hours or until the top is golden and the cake has a gentle wobble. Cool to room temperature in the pan, then refrigerate and chill completely.

Dust with icing sugar, cut into slices and serve. **Serves 6-8**

Date night

What do they say about the way to a man's heart?
Everyone should have a date night once in a while where you
treat yourself and someone special to a memorable meal.

Double dip

Double dipping is usually taboo... but not when you create a dip for two.

500g thick Greek-style
   yoghurt
1 tbs lemon juice
Seeds of 1 pomegranate
Slivered pistachios*,
   extra virgin olive oil,
   crackers and crudités
   (such as radishes and
   heirloom carrots*),
   to serve

Begin this recipe the day before.

Combine the yoghurt and lemon juice in a bowl. Place a large sieve over a bowl, making sure it doesn't touch the base. Line with muslin or a clean Chux cloth, leaving enough overhanging the sides to cover. Place yoghurt in the sieve, draw the muslin over the top, cover with plastic wrap and refrigerate overnight.

Discard any liquid that has drained from the yoghurt and season. Spoon into a serving dish, then scatter with pomegranate seeds and slivered pistachios. Drizzle with extra virgin olive oil and serve with crackers and crudités. **Serves 2-4**

* Slivered pistachios are from Middle Eastern food shops and gourmet food shops. Heirloom carrots are from farmers' markets and selected greengrocers.

Champagne & asparagus risotto with oysters

30g unsalted butter

1 tbs extra virgin olive oil,
   plus extra to drizzle

1 leek, trimmed, finely
   chopped

2 garlic cloves,
   finely chopped

300g carnaroli*
   or arborio rice

1 cup (250ml) Champagne,
   plus extra to serve

1L (4 cups) chicken stock
   (see 'Basics', p 296),
   heated

2 bunches thin asparagus,
   woody ends trimmed

1/3 cup (25g) finely grated
   parmesan

2 tbs mascarpone

2 tbs finely chopped
   flat-leaf parsley

12 oysters, freshly shucked

Lemon wedges, to serve

Melt the butter and oil in a saucepan over low heat. Add the leek and cook, stirring, for 5 minutes until softened. Add the garlic and cook for a further 1 minute. Add the rice and cook for 1 minute, stirring to coat the grains.

Increase heat to medium and add the Champagne, then simmer for 1-2 minutes until the liquid has almost evaporated. Stir in the stock, a ladleful at a time, allowing each to be absorbed before adding the next. Continue to cook, stirring constantly, for 20 minutes or until al dente. Just before adding the last ladleful of stock, stir through the asparagus, then cook for 2 minutes until tender.

To serve, stir in the parmesan, mascarpone and parsley, then drizzle with extra oil and season. Serve with freshly shucked oysters, lemon wedges and a glass of Champagne. **Serves 4**

* Carnaroli rice is available from gourmet food shops and delis.

Two Hearts Waltz:

Lamb en croute

30g unsalted butter

150g Swiss brown
  mushrooms, chopped

3 chicken livers, trimmed,
  finely chopped

4 eschalots, finely chopped

2 garlic cloves,
  finely chopped

1½ bunches English spinach,
  chopped

2 tbs toasted pine nuts,
  chopped

2 tbs olive oil

2 x 200g lamb backstraps,
  trimmed

1 cup (250ml) red wine

1 cup (250ml) beef
  or veal stock∗

¼ cup (80g) redcurrant jelly

2 sheets frozen puff
  pastry, thawed

1 egg, lightly beaten

Steamed green beans,
  to serve

Preheat the oven to 200°C.

Melt the butter in a frypan over medium-high heat. Add the mushrooms, chicken liver, eschalot and garlic to the pan, and cook for 2-3 minutes until the mushrooms are softened and the liver is sealed. Add the spinach and cook, stirring, for 1 minute or until wilted. Season and cool slightly. Transfer to a food processor, pulse a few times to form a coarse paste, then stir through the pine nuts. Transfer to a bowl, cover and refrigerate until cold.

Heat the oil in a frypan over high heat. Season the lamb, then add to the pan and cook, turning for 2-3 minutes or until brown all over. Remove the lamb from the pan and set aside to cool.

Add the red wine to the frypan and simmer for 2-3 minutes until slightly reduced. Add the stock and redcurrant jelly and cook, stirring, for 5-6 minutes or until reduced and thick. Keep warm and set aside.

Spread one-quarter of the spinach mixture over two-thirds of 1 puff pastry sheet, leaving a 3cm border. Place 1 lamb backstrap on the spinach mixture, then cover the lamb with another quarter of the spinach mixture. Tuck in the sides of the pastry, then fold over the pastry to enclose the filling. Trim the pastry, then press down to seal the edges. Repeat with remaining pastry, spinach mixture and lamb.

Cut any excess pastry into leaf shapes, if desired, and place on top of the lamb parcels. Brush the pastry with egg. Place on a baking tray and bake for 12-15 minutes until golden. Remove from the oven and set aside to rest for 5 minutes.

Slice the lamb en croute and serve with the redcurrant sauce and steamed green beans. **Serves 4**

∗ Veal stock is available from selected delis and butchers.

Lobster spaghetti

I love the scene in *Lady and the Tramp* where they share a plate of spaghetti. This special occasion dish is sure to inspire a bit of romance.

500g vine-ripened tomatoes
1 cooked lobster*
100ml extra virgin olive oil
2 garlic cloves,
   finely chopped
5cm-piece fresh ginger,
   finely grated
50ml dry white wine
¼ cup (60ml) thickened
   cream
Finely grated zest
   of ½ lemon, plus
   1 tbs lemon juice
4 spring onions, thinly sliced
2 tbs finely chopped
   flat-leaf parsley
250g spaghetti

Cut a small cross in the base of each tomato and place in a bowl. Pour over enough boiling water to cover and stand for 1 minute, then drain and refresh in cold water. Peel the tomatoes, then scoop out the seeds and roughly chop. Set aside.

Cut the lobster in half, then scoop out the meat and cut into chunks. Set aside.

Heat the oil in a frypan over medium heat. Add the garlic and cook, stirring, for 30 seconds or until fragrant. Add the ginger and white wine and cook for 2-3 minutes until the wine has almost evaporated. Add the tomato, season well and cook, stirring occasionally, for 5 minutes or until the tomato breaks down. Reduce heat to low, then add the lobster meat, cream, lemon zest and juice, and most of the spring onion, stirring until just warmed though. Remove from heat, stir in most of the parsley and season.

Meanwhile, cook pasta in boiling salted water according to the packet instructions until al dente. Drain.

Toss the pasta with the lobster sauce and divide among bowls. Garnish with the remaining spring onion and parsley and serve. **Serves 2**

* Cooked lobster is from fishmongers and selected supermarkets.

Heirloom tomato pastry hearts

1 sheet frozen puff
   pastry, thawed
⅓ cup (80g) fresh ricotta
2 tbs (40g) mascarpone
2 tbs finely grated parmesan
1 egg, beaten
2 tsp thyme leaves
200g heirloom
   cherry tomatoes*
Rocket leaves and balsamic
   vinegar, to serve

Preheat the oven to 180°C. Line a baking tray with baking paper.

Using a 10cm heart-shaped pastry cutter, cut the pastry into 4 hearts. Carefully cut a 2cm border into 2 hearts, then discard the inner pastry heart, reserving the heart-shaped borders. Brush the borders with water, then arrange the borders, watered-side down, on top of the whole pastry hearts, gently pressing down to seal. Transfer to the baking tray and set aside.

Combine ricotta, mascarpone, parmesan and most of the egg. Season, then stir in the thyme leaves. Spoon the cheese mixture into the centre of the hearts and place the tomatoes on top. Use the remaining egg to brush the pastry border.

Bake for 8-10 minutes until pastry is golden and the filling is set. Scatter with rocket, drizzle with balsamic vinegar and serve. **Serves 2**

* Heirloom cherry tomatoes are available from farmers' markets and selected greengrocers.

Let's run away to Paris
and never come back.

Chateaubriand with bearnaise and drunken potatoes

This is rustic and romantic – the perfect roast dinner to share.

¼ cup (60ml) olive oil

400g desiree potatoes, peeled

1 cup (250ml) white wine

2 thyme sprigs, leaves picked

2 garlic cloves, sliced

400g centre-cut chateaubriand beef*, trussed

Bearnaise sauce

¼ cup (60ml) white wine vinegar

¼ cup (60ml) white wine

2 eschalots, finely chopped

¼ cup finely chopped tarragon

3 egg yolks

200g unsalted butter, melted, heated

Preheat the oven to 180°C.

Grease a baking tray with 1 tablespoon olive oil. Thinly slice the potatoes (a mandoline is ideal) and arrange on the oiled baking tray in a single layer, slightly overlapping so there are no gaps. Pour over the wine and scatter with the half the thyme leaves, then season. Bake for 1 hour or until all of the wine has been absorbed and the potatoes are tender and golden. Keep warm.

Meanwhile, combine the garlic, and remaining thyme and 2 tablespoons olive oil. Rub the oil mixture into the beef to coat well and stand at room temperature for 30 minutes.

Heat a frypan over medium-high. Season the beef, then cook, turning, for 3-4 minutes until browned on all sides. Transfer to a baking tray and bake for 10 minutes. Remove from the oven, then rest, loosely covered with foil, for 5 minutes.

Meanwhile, for the bearnaise sauce, place the vinegar, wine, eschalot and 1 tablespoon tarragon in a saucepan over medium heat and simmer until reduced to 2 tablespoons. Place in a blender with the egg yolks and blend to combine. With the motor running, slowly drizzle in the hot melted butter, blending until a smooth emulsion. Season and stir through the remaining tarragon.

Cut the beef into slices and serve with the drunken potatoes and bearnaise sauce. **Serves 2**

* Chateaubriand beef is available from butchers.

Quail with rose petals and yoghurt

4 garlic cloves,
  finely chopped
2 tsp mixed spice
2 tsp ground cumin
⅓ cup (80ml) rosewater
⅓ cup (80ml) lemon juice
¼ cup (60ml) extra
  virgin olive oil
½ cup (160g) rose-petal
  jelly* or quince paste,
  plus extra to serve
8 quails*, butterflied
Thick Greek-style yoghurt,
  dried edible rose petals*
  and rocket leaves, to serve

Place the garlic and half each of the spices, rosewater, lemon juice and oil in a dish. Coat the quail in the marinade, then cover and refrigerate for at least 4 hours or overnight.

Place the remaining spices, rosewater, lemon juice and oil in a saucepan over low heat with the rose-petal jelly and warm gently, stirring until the jelly is melted and smooth. Set aside.

Preheat a chargrill pan or barbecue to medium-high heat.

Season the quail and cook for 3-4 minutes each side until charred and cooked through. Divide quail among serving plates, drizzle with the rose-petal sauce and yoghurt and scatter with rose petals and rocket leaves. Serve with extra rose-petal jelly. **Serves 4**

✳ Quail is available from selected butchers; ask your butcher to butterfly the quail. Rose-petal jelly and dried rose petals are available from Middle Eastern food shops and gourmet food shops.

Passion cake

Pulp from 8 passionfruits
  (to give about 200ml
  passionfruit pulp)
100g desiccated coconut
¾ cup (165g) caster sugar
½ cup (75g) plain flour,
  sifted
4 eggs, lightly beaten
125g unsalted butter,
  melted
1 tsp lemon juice
Raspberries, to serve

Passionfruit icing
50g unsalted butter,
  softened
3 cups (450g) icing
  sugar, sifted
Pulp from 3 passionfruits
  (to give about ¼ cup
  passionfruit pulp)

Preheat the oven to 180°C. Grease and line an 18cm x 16cm heart-shaped cake pan or 18cm round springform cake pan.

Place the passionfruit pulp in a food processor and pulse several times to loosen the pulp from the seeds. Set aside.

Combine coconut, sugar and flour in a bowl. Fold the eggs, butter, lemon juice and passionfruit pulp and seeds, then fold together until combined. Pour into the cake pan and bake for 35-40 minutes until a skewer inserted into the centre comes out clean. Cool in the pan for 5 minutes, then turn out onto a wire rack to cool completely.

For the passionfruit icing, place the butter and icing sugar in an electric mixer. Beat until doubled in size, then add the passionfruit pulp, mixing well until combined.

Spread the icing over the cooled cake, then decorate with the raspberries and serve. **Serves 4**

Chocolatini with chocolate 'body paint'

This silky chocolate 'body paint' is simply seductive
when poured over ice cream or fresh berries.

½ cup (125ml) chocolate
   liqueur
100ml vodka
2 tbs grated dark chocolate

Chocolate 'body paint'
300ml pure (thin) cream
60g unsalted butter
1 firmly packed cup (250g)
   brown sugar
½ cup (50g) cocoa
100g good-quality dark
   chocolate, chopped
½ tsp vanilla extract

For the chocolate 'body paint', place cream and butter in a saucepan over low heat, stirring, until butter has melted. Add the sugar, stirring until dissolved. Bring to just below boiling point, then remove from heat. Sift in the cocoa, then add the chocolate and vanilla, stirring until the chocolate has melted. Cool, then pour into sterilised jars. The chocolate 'body paint' can be kept refrigerated for up to 2 weeks and gently reheated before serving.

For the chocolatinis, place chocolate liqueur and vodka in a cocktail shaker with plenty of ice and shake to combine. Strain into martini glasses and sprinkle with grated chocolate. **Makes 2**

Baked custards

600ml pure (thin) cream
300ml milk
¼ cup (55g) caster sugar
3 eggs
1 tsp vanilla extract
A few drops of pink food
  colouring (optional)
Icing sugar, to serve

Preheat the oven to 140°C.

Combine the cream, milk, sugar, eggs, vanilla and pink food colouring in a bowl, lightly whisking to combine. Strain through a fine sieve into a jug, then pour into six 200ml ramekins. Place the ramekins in a roasting pan and pour enough boiling water into the pan to come halfway up the sides of the ramekins.

Bake for 1-1¼ hours until the custards have set, but still have a slight wobble. Cool slightly, then refrigerate.

To serve, cut a heart shape slightly smaller than the top of the ramekins from a square of baking paper. Sit the baking paper square over a custard and dust with icing sugar. Repeat with the remaining custards and serve. **Makes 6**

Get cosy

These are the sorts of dishes you'll want to cook all winter long. They melt in the mouth, warm the heart and fill your home with rich aromas. So light the fire and open your favourite bottle of red.

3753 K°ODAK

Warm barley & mushroom salad with Taleggio

⅔ cup (150g) pearl barley

10g dried porcini
   mushrooms*

50g unsalted butter

⅓ cup (80ml) extra virgin
   olive oil

1 garlic clove, finely chopped

350g mixed wild mushrooms
   (such as chestnut, shiitake
   and Swiss browns), sliced
   or left whole

⅓ cup finely chopped
   flat-leaf parsley leaves

2 tbs chopped chives

⅓ cup finely chopped
   mint leaves

1 tbs red wine vinegar

1 bunch rocket

150g Taleggio cheese*,
   sliced

Place the barley in a saucepan of cold water over medium-high heat. Bring to the boil, then reduce the heat to low and cook for 1 hour or until the barley is tender, topping up the water if necessary. Drain.

Meanwhile, soak the porcini in ½ cup (125ml) boiling water for 10 minutes. Drain, reserving the soaking liquid, then roughly chop the porcini and set aside.

Melt the butter with 1 tablespoon oil in a frypan over medium heat. Add the garlic and wild mushrooms, then cook, stirring occasionally, for 3-4 minutes until tender. Add the porcini and soaking liquid, then cook for a further 2-3 minutes until most of the liquid has been absorbed. Toss the mushrooms and herbs with the barley and season. Keep warm.

Whisk the remaining ¼ cup (60ml) olive oil with the red wine vinegar, season, then toss with the rocket.

Fold the Taleggio through the warm barley salad, then divide among plates. Top with the dressed rocket and serve. **Serves 6**

* Dried porcini mushrooms and Taleggio cheese (an Italian wash-rind cheese) are available from delis.

Cauliflower cheese soup

30g unsalted butter

1½ tbs olive oil

1 onion, chopped

1 garlic clove, chopped

1 leek, trimmed, sliced

1 small cauliflower,
    broken into florets

3 cups (750ml) chicken stock
    (see 'Basics', p 296)

100g grated cheddar

1-2 tsp wholegrain mustard

300ml thickened cream

4 slices flat pancetta*
    or bacon

½ cup (35g) fresh
    breadcrumbs

2 tbs chopped chives

Cheddar wafers

¾ cup (90g) finely
    grated cheddar

2 tbs flour

Preheat the oven to 180°C. Line 2 large baking trays with foil.

Melt the butter with 1 tablespoon oil in a frypan over medium heat Cook the onion, garlic and leek, stirring, for 3-4 minutes until soft but not coloured. Add the cauliflower and stock, bring to a boil, then reduce the heat to medium-low and simmer for 20 minutes or until the cauliflower is tender. Cool slightly, then stir in the cheddar, mustard and half the cream.

In batches, blend the cauliflower soup until smooth. Return to a clean saucepan. Add the remaining 150ml cream, season, then stir over low heat to warm through.

Meanwhile, for the cheddar wafers, combine the cheddar and flour in a bowl and season. Place twelve 5cm rounds of the cheddar mixture on the lined baking trays, leaving room between each to spread. Bake for 5-6 minutes until golden. Set aside to cool.

Place the pancetta on a baking tray and bake for 6-8 minutes until crispy. Cool slightly, then break into small pieces.

Place the breadcrumbs on a baking tray and drizzle with remaining 2 teaspoons oil. Place in the oven and bake for 5-6 minutes until golden and crispy.

Ladle soup into serving bowls, then top with the pancetta, chives and breadcrumbs. Serve soup with the cheddar wafers. **Serves 4-6**

* Flat pancetta is available from delis.

Chilli for a crowd

½ cup (125ml) olive oil
1 onion, finely chopped
2 star anise
2 garlic cloves,
   finely chopped
1 green chilli, seeds
   removed, finely chopped
1kg beef mince
2 tbs tomato paste
3 tsp ground cumin
1 tsp chilli powder
2 tsp smoked paprika
   (pimenton)
350ml red wine
1 tbs Worcestershire sauce
1½ cups (375ml) beef stock
400g can chopped tomatoes
400g can red kidney beans,
   rinsed, drained
1 long red chilli, seeds
   removed, finely shredded
Grated cheddar, sour cream,
   mashed avocado and
   tortilla chips, to serve

Preheat the oven to 170°C.

Heat the oil in a large ovenproof saucepan or flameproof casserole over medium heat. Add the onion and star anise and cook, stirring, for 3-4 minutes until softened. Add the garlic and green chilli and cook, stirring, for 30 seconds or until fragrant. Add the beef and cook, breaking up any lumps with a wooden spoon, for 5-6 minutes until browned. Add the tomato paste and spices and cook, stirring, for 1-2 minutes. Pour in the wine, bring to a simmer, then cook for 4-6 minutes until reduced by half. Add the Worcestershire sauce, stock and tomato, then season well. Bring to the boil then cover with a lid and transfer to the oven. Bake for 1 hour or until the chilli is reduced and thick.

Stir the beans into the chilli and top with shredded red chilli. Serve chilli with cheese, sour cream, avocado and tortilla chips. **Serves 8-10**

Massaman curry lamb shanks

2 tbs sunflower oil

6 French-trimmed
   lamb shanks

1 onion, finely chopped

⅓ cup (100g) massaman
   curry paste

1 tbs palm sugar*
   or brown sugar

3 kaffir lime leaves*

400ml coconut cream

2 cups (500ml) beef stock

500g baby chat potatoes,
   peeled, halved if large

1 cup (120g) frozen peas

2 tbs lime juice

2 tbs fish sauce

Coriander leaves and
   steamed jasmine rice,
   to serve

Preheat the oven to 180°C.

Heat 1 tablespoon oil in a large flameproof casserole over medium-high heat. Season the lamb shanks, then in batches, cook the lamb, turning, for 3-4 minutes until browned all over. Set the shanks aside.

Reduce the heat to medium, then add remaining 1 tablespoon oil to the pan. Cook the onion, stirring, for 2-3 minutes until softened. Add the curry paste and cook, stirring, for 1-2 minutes until fragrant. Stir in the sugar, kaffir lime leaves, coconut cream and stock, then return the lamb to the pan. Increase the heat to high and bring to the boil. Cover, then transfer to the oven. Bake for 1 hour.

Add the potato and cook for a further 30 minutes or until the lamb and potatoes are tender. Add the peas and bake for a further 10 minutes or until peas are tender.

Stir through lime juice and fish sauce and season to taste. Serve the lamb shanks with coriander and steamed rice. **Serves 6**

* Palm sugar and kaffir lime leaves are available from Asian food shops.

Chinese braised beef

2 tbs plain flour
1 tsp five-spice powder
1kg boneless beef shin*,
  cut into 5cm pieces
¼ cup (60ml) peanut
  or sunflower oil
1 onion, finely chopped
4 garlic cloves, sliced
3cm piece of ginger,
  peeled, grated
½ bunch spring onions,
  finely chopped, plus
  extra shredded spring
  onion to serve
1 long red chilli, seeds
  removed, finely chopped,
  plus extra shredded
  chilli to serve
50g Chinese rock sugar*
  or brown sugar
¼ cup (60ml) Chinese rice
  wine (shaohsing)*
1 cinnamon quill
¼ cup (60ml) dark soy sauce
1L (4 cups) beef consomme
2 tbs peanut butter
2 tbs hoisin sauce
Steamed bok choy and
  steamed Chinese buns*,
  to serve

Combine the flour and five-spice powder with 1 teaspoon salt. Coat the beef in the flour mixture, shaking off and reserving any excess flour.

Heat 2 tablespoons oil in a flameproof casserole over medium-high heat. In batches, cook the beef, turning, for 3-4 minutes until browned all over. Remove from the pan and set aside.

Add the remaining 1 tablespoon oil to the pan and cook the onion, stirring, for 1-2 minutes until softened. Add the garlic, ginger, spring onion and chilli, then cook, stirring, for a further 1 minute. Stir in the reserved flour mixture with the sugar, rice wine, cinnamon, soy sauce, consomme, peanut butter and hoisin sauce. Return the beef to the pan, then increase heat to medium-high and bring to the boil. Cover and transfer to the oven. Bake for 2 hours or until the beef is tender.

Top the braised beef with shredded spring onion and chilli, then serve with the steamed bok choy and Chinese buns.

* Beef shin is available from butchers; substitute chuck steak. Chinese rock sugar, Chinese rice wine (shaohsing) and Chinese buns are available from Asian food shops.

Beat the chill

with hearty comfort food.

Fish pie

There is nothing more comforting than a wonderful fish pie.
Rich and creamy, it really hits the spot on cold nights.

2 cups (500ml) milk
1 small onion, halved
2 fresh bay leaves*
3 thyme sprigs
1kg desiree or pontiac
    potatoes, peeled, chopped
100g unsalted butter
300ml thickened cream
500g skinless salmon fillet,
    pin-boned, chopped into
    3cm pieces
500g skinless white fish
    fillet (such as blue-eye or
    ling), pin-boned, chopped
    into 3cm pieces
½ cup (125ml) fish stock
40g plain flour
¼ cup finely chopped
    flat-leaf parsley,
    plus extra to serve
250g peeled green prawns
3 hard-boiled eggs, chopped

Place milk, onion, bay leaves and thyme in a saucepan over medium-high heat. Bring to just below boiling point, then stand for 30 minutes to infuse. Strain into a jug, discarding the solids.

Meanwhile, preheat the oven to 180°C.

Place the potato in a saucepan of cold salted water, bring to the boil, then reduce heat to medium-high and cook for 12 minutes or until tender. Drain well. Pass through a potato ricer or mash well in a bowl. Add 50g butter and 200ml cream, season, then mix until smooth. Keep warm.

Place the salmon and white fish in a 1.5L baking dish and pour over the fish stock. Season and cover with foil. Bake for 15 minutes or until the fish is cooked through. Using a slotted spoon, transfer the fish to a bowl, reserving ⅓ cup (80ml) cooking liquid.

Melt 40g butter in a pan over medium-low heat. Add the flour and cook, stirring, for 1 minute. Gradually whisk the infused milk into the pan, then reduce the heat to low and whisk for 2-3 minutes until thickened. Whisk the reserved cooking liquid into the bechamel sauce with the remaining 100ml cream. Stir in the parsley and season.

Return the fish to the baking dish and scatter over the prawns and chopped egg. Pour over the bechamel sauce, then top with the mashed potato, smoothing out the surface with the back of a large spoon. Dot with the remaining 10g butter.

Increase the oven to 200°C. Bake the pie for 20-25 minutes until bubbling and golden. Sprinkle with extra parsley and serve. **Serves 6**

* Fresh bay leaves are from selected greengrocers.

Duck cassoulet

This easy version of a classic French dish uses ready-prepared confit duck legs.

2 tbs olive oil

2 onions, thinly sliced

150g pancetta,
  cut into thin strips

3 tsp thyme leaves

2 garlic cloves, sliced

1 cup (250ml) dry white wine

2 x 400g cans chopped
  tomatoes

1 bay leaf

1 cup (120g) pitted
  green olives

2 x 400g cans cannellini
  beans, rinsed, drained

4 confit duck legs*

50g unsalted butter

1½ cups (105g) fresh
  breadcrumbs

2 tbs chopped parsley

Mixed salad leaves, to serve

Preheat the oven to 180°C.

Heat the oil in a large saucepan over medium heat. Add the onion and pancetta, then cook, stirring, for 3-4 minutes until the onion has softened. Add the thyme, garlic and white wine, increase the heat to medium-high and bring to the boil. Simmer for 3-4 minutes until reduced by half. Add the tomato and bay leaf and cook for a further 10-12 minutes until reduced by one-third. Stir in the olives and cannellini beans. Season and set aside.

Scrape off any excess fat from the duck legs. (The duck fat can be kept in an airtight container in the fridge for up to 2 months. You can use it to roast potatoes.) Place the duck legs in a baking dish, pour over the sauce and cover with foil. Bake for 20 minutes or until the duck is warmed through.

Meanwhile, melt the butter in a frypan over medium heat. Add the breadcrumbs and cook, stirring, for 2-3 minutes until golden. Season, then remove from the heat and stir through the parsley.

Remove the cassoulet from the oven, scatter with the breadcrumbs, then bake for a further 10 minutes or until the breadcrumbs are crispy.

Divide the duck cassoulet among plates and serve with mixed salad leaves. **Serves 4**

* Confit duck legs are available from gourmet food shops, poultry shops and selected butchers.

Self-saucing chocolate pudding

60g unsalted butter
½ cup (125ml) milk
1 tsp vanilla extract
¾ cup (165g) caster sugar
1 cup (150g) self-raising
  flour, sifted
2 tbs cocoa, sifted,
  plus extra to dust
¾ firmly packed cup
  (185g) brown sugar
Thick cream, to serve

Preheat the oven to 180°C. Grease a 1.5L ovenproof baking dish.

Melt the butter with the milk in a saucepan over low heat. Add the vanilla, caster sugar, flour and 1 tablespoon cocoa, stirring to combine, then spread into the baking dish.

Combine the brown sugar and remaining 1 tablespoon cocoa in a bowl with 2 cups (500ml) boiling water. Stir until sugar has dissolved, then carefully pour over the pudding batter. Bake for 35-40 minutes until the top is firm. Stand for 5 minutes.

Dust with cocoa and serve with thick cream. **Serves 4-6**

Jam & chocolate roly poly with proper custard

This is so far removed from the roly polys we used to be served at school. With some proper custard, it makes a lovely grown-up winter dessert.

1 cup (150g) self-raising
    flour
2 tbs caster sugar
75g powdered suet mix*
100ml milk
1 cup (320g) good-quality
    raspberry jam
½ cup (90g) chopped
    dark chocolate
Proper custard (see 'Basics',
    p 296), to serve

Sift the flour into a bowl, then stir in the sugar, suet and ½ teaspoon salt. Add the milk and stir to form a soft dough. On a lightly floured surface, roll the dough out to a 20cm x 30cm rectangle. Spread with the jam, leaving a 2cm border on all sides. Scatter with the chocolate, then roll up tightly from the long side to form a long roll.

Lightly grease a sheet of baking paper, then place the roly poly, seam-side down, on the baking paper. Fold in the ends and tuck underneath the roll. Wrap in foil, twisting the ends to seal.

Place the roly poly in a large steamer or fish kettle and steam for 45 minutes, topping up the water, if necessary. To test if it's cooked, pull back the foil and baking paper – the roly poly should spring back when lightly touched. Remove from the steamer and stand for 10 minutes.

Remove the foil and baking paper from the roly poly and cut into thick slices. Serve with warm custard. **Serves 6-8**

* Powdered suet mix is available from the baking aisle in supermarkets.

Chocolate & rum bread & butter pudding

½ cup (80g) sultanas

⅓ cup (80ml) dark rum

300g brioche loaf*,
  thinly sliced

60g unsalted butter,
  softened

100g dark chocolate,
  chopped

4 eggs

½ cup (110g) caster sugar

300ml pure (thin) cream,
  plus extra to serve

½ cup (125ml) milk

1 tsp vanilla extract

Icing sugar, to dust

Grease a 1.5L ceramic baking dish. Place the sultanas and rum in a bowl and stand for 30 minutes.

Spread one side of each brioche slice with the butter. Arrange half the brioche in the baking dish, buttered-side up, and sprinkle with half each of the chocolate, soaked sultanas and soaking rum. Repeat the layers.

Whisk the eggs, sugar, cream, milk and vanilla together in a bowl until combined. Strain, then pour over the pudding. Stand for 30 minutes to allow the egg mixture to soak into the brioche and the flavours to develop.

Preheat the oven to 170°C.

Place the pudding in a deep roasting pan. Pour enough boiling water into the pan to come halfway up the sides of the baking dish. Bake for 1 hour or until the custard has set (cover loosely with foil if the pudding is browning too quickly). Remove the pudding from the roasting pan and stand for 10 minutes.

Dust with icing sugar and serve with extra cream. **Serves 6-8**

* Brioche is from selected supermarkets or order from your baker.

Playing with fire

There's no better way to transform ordinary food into meals bursting
with flavour than cooking it over fire, and with these simple recipes,
you won't have to wait until the weekend to light the barbecue.

Haloumi with Mediterranean salad

I always feel vegetarians have less to get excited about at barbecues, but this flavoursome dish will make a satisfying main at your next alfresco feast.

200g fregola*

6 roma tomatoes (about 360g),
  seeds removed, chopped

12 pitted kalamata olives,
  chopped

12 pitted green olives,
  chopped

6 marinated artichokes,
  drained, chopped

1 spring onion, finely chopped

1 tbs baby capers,
  rinsed, drained

1 preserved lemon quarter*,
  white pith removed,
  rind finely chopped

30g toasted pine nuts

¼ cup mint leaves, plus
  extra leaves to garnish

1 tbs chopped flat-leaf parsley

1 tbs chopped basil

250g haloumi cheese,
  cut into wedges

¼ cup (60ml) extra virgin
  olive oil, plus extra to brush

2 tbs lemon juice, plus
  lemon wedges to serve

Cook the fregola according to packet instructions, then place in a bowl and toss with the tomato, olives, artichokes, spring onion, capers, preserved lemon rind, pine nuts and herbs. Set aside.

Preheat a chargrill pan or barbecue to medium-high heat.

Rinse the haloumi under cold water to remove any excess salt, then pat dry with paper towel and brush with olive oil. Grill for 1 minute each side until crispy and golden. Keep warm.

Whisk the oil and lemon juice together, season, then drizzle over the salad and toss to combine. Top the salad with the haloumi, garnish with extra mint leaves and serve with lemon wedges. **Serves 4**

✱ Fregola (small Sardinian pasta) and preserved lemon quarters are available from delis.

Barbecue tapas

My good friend Matt Preston taught me how to make this dish. With chorizo as the star ingredient, this is an easy recipe to kick things off.

Large pinch of saffron
threads
½ tsp coriander seeds
½ tsp cumin seeds
½ tsp fennel seeds
1 tsp sweet paprika
2 garlic cloves, chopped
¼ cup chopped
oregano leaves
2 tsp red wine vinegar
1 tbs olive oil
2 x 170g skinless chicken
breast fillets, cut
into 3cm pieces
4 chorizo sausages
400g can chopped tomatoes
2 tbs finely chopped
flat-leaf parsley

Soak the saffron in 1 tablespoon boiling water for 10 minutes.

Meanwhile, place the coriander, cumin and fennel seeds in a dry frypan over low heat and cook, stirring, for 1 minute or until fragrant. Transfer to a mortar and pestle and pound until coarsely ground. Add the paprika, garlic, oregano, vinegar, saffron and soaking liquid, and 2 teaspoons oil, then pound until a coarse paste. Transfer to a bowl and season, then add the chicken, tossing to coat well in the mixture. Cover and refrigerate for 2 hours to marinate.

Preheat the barbecue to medium heat.

Cut the chorizo on the diagonal into 2cm-thick slices and cook on the hotplate for 2 minutes each side until crispy and golden. Move the chorizo to one side of the hotplate to keep warm. Pour the tomato onto the hotplate, season well, and cook for 2-3 minutes until the juices have reduced and thickened. Toss with the chorizo and parsley. Keep warm.

Increase the heat to medium-high and brush the barbecue with remaining 2 teaspoons oil. Cook the chicken for 6-8 minutes, turning, until cooked through. Serve the chicken with the chorizo. **Serves 4**

Spicy prawns with harissa couscous

2 small red chillies,
   seeds removed, chopped
Juice of ½ lemon
3 garlic cloves
1 tbs smoked paprika
   (pimenton)
⅓ cup (80ml) olive oil
1 tbs red wine vinegar
16 large green prawns

Harissa couscous
1 cup (200g) couscous
1 tsp harissa*
1 tbs pomegranate
   molasses*
2 tsp baharat spice mix*
Juice of ½ lemon
1 red onion, thinly sliced
Seeds of 1 pomegranate
2 cups coriander leaves

Place chilli, lemon juice, garlic, paprika, oil and vinegar in a mini food processor and whiz until you have a smooth paste. Coat the prawns in the marinade, cover and refrigerate for 1 hour.

For the harissa couscous, place the couscous in a bowl and pour over 400ml boiling water. Stir to combine, then add the harissa, pomegranate molasses, baharat and lemon juice. Season with salt, then cover and set aside for 10 minutes or until the water is absorbed. Fluff the couscous with a fork and stir through the onion, pomegranate seeds and coriander leaves. Set aside.

Meanwhile, preheat a chargrill pan or barbecue to medium-high heat.

Cook the prawns for 2 minutes each side or until just cooked through. Serve the prawns with the harissa couscous. **Serves 4**

* Harissa (a North African chilli paste), pomegranate molasses and baharat spice mix are available from Middle Eastern food shops and selected delis.

Chermoula fish with tahini sauce

1 tsp cumin seeds

1 tsp coriander seeds

1 tsp smoked paprika (pimenton)

¼ tsp dried chilli flakes

1 tbs finely grated ginger

2 tsp ground turmeric

2 garlic cloves, roughly chopped

2 cups flat-leaf parsley leaves

2 cups coriander leaves

Finely grated zest of 2 lemons, plus juice of 4 lemons

4 x 200g skinless barramundi fillets or other firm white fish

½ cup (140g) tahini*

Olive oil, to brush

Rocket leaves and mint leaves, to serve

Place the cumin and coriander seeds in a small frypan over medium heat. Cook, stirring, for 1 minute until fragrant. Transfer to a mini food processor with the smoked paprika, chilli flakes, ginger, turmeric, garlic, parsley, coriander leaves, zest and juice of 2 lemons, and 1 teaspoon salt. Whiz until a thick paste. Coat the fish in the chermoula marinade and set aside for 15 minutes.

Meanwhile, combine the juice of remaining 2 lemons with the tahini and ½ cup (125ml) water and season. Set aside.

Preheat a chargrill pan or barbecue to medium-high heat.

Brush the chargrill pan or barbecue with oil and cook the fish for 3-4 minutes each side until cooked through. Transfer to serving plates, drizzle with the tahini cream sauce and serve with rocket and mint leaves. **Serves 4**

✱ Tahini is available from health food shops and selected supermarkets.

Beef on lemongrass skewers with cucumber salad

These lemongrass skewers add a distinct Asian flavour to the beef as it cooks.

4 x 200g beef eye fillets
3 lemongrass stems
Sunflower oil, to brush

Marinade
¼ cup (60ml) peanut oil
½ red onion, chopped
2 garlic cloves, chopped
2 tbs chopped coriander
2 kaffir lime leaves*,
　thinly sliced
2 tsp ground turmeric
1 tsp ground cumin
2 tbs soy sauce
1 tsp palm sugar*
1 tbs lime juice

Cucumber salad
3 Lebanese cucumbers
¼ cup (65g) palm sugar*
¼ cup (60ml) lime juice,
　plus extra wedges to serve
2 small red chillies, seeds
　removed, finely chopped
4 eschalots, thinly sliced
1 tbs fish sauce
¼ cup (35g) roasted
　peanuts, chopped

For the marinade, place all the ingredients in a mini food processor and whiz until a smooth paste. Transfer to a bowl. Cut the beef into 4cm chunks, then coat well in the marinade. Cover and refrigerate for 1 hour.

Meanwhile, for the cucumber salad, slice the cucumbers into thin strips, place in a sieve and sprinkle with salt. Leave over the sink for 20 minutes to drain, then rinse and pat dry with paper towel. Combine palm sugar, lime juice, chilli, eschalot and fish sauce in a bowl, stirring until the sugar has dissolved. Season to taste and set aside.

Cut the lemongrass into 15cm lengths. Thread the beef onto the lemongrass skewers and bring to room temperature.

Preheat a chargrill pan or barbecue to medium-high heat.

Brush the chargrill pan or barbecue hotplate with oil and cook the skewers, turning, for 4-5 minutes until lightly charred on the outside, but still rare in the centre. Remove the beef skewers from the heat and allow to rest, loosely covered with foil, for 5 minutes.

Toss the cucumber with the palm sugar dressing and stir through the peanuts. Serve the skewers with the cucumber salad. **Serves 4**

* Kaffir lime leaves and palm sugar are from Asian food shops.

I love the *smoky aroma*
of food cooked over coals.

Lamb burgers with harissa mayonnaise and orange relish

1 tsp ground cumin
1 tsp ground coriander
1 tsp ground turmeric
1 tsp cinnamon
1 tbs honey
1kg lamb mince
½ red onion, finely chopped
3 garlic cloves,
    finely chopped
4 crusty bread rolls,
    split, toasted
Micro salad leaves*, to serve

Harissa mayonnaise
½ cup (150g) whole-egg
    mayonnaise
2 tbs harissa*
2 tbs finely chopped
    coriander

Orange relish
1 orange, peeled, pith
    removed, chopped
1 cup (120g) pitted
    kalamata olives, sliced
1 tbs slivered pistachios*

Combine spices, honey, lamb, onion and garlic in a bowl and season. Divide the mixture into 4 portions, then use damp hands to form into burgers. Refrigerate for 30 minutes or until firm.

Meanwhile, for the harissa mayonnaise, combine the mayonnaise, harissa and coriander in a bowl and season. Cover and keep chilled until ready to serve.

For the orange relish, place the orange, olive and pistachios in a bowl and toss to combine. Set aside.

Preheat a chargrill pan or barbecue to medium-high heat

Grill the burgers for 4-5 minutes each side until cooked through. Spread the base of each bread roll with the harissa mayonnaise. Add the lamb burger, then top with the orange relish and micro salad leaves and serve. **Makes 4**

* Micro salad leaves are available from farmers' markets and selected greengrocers. Harissa (a North African chilli paste) and slivered pistachios are available from gourmet food shops.

Sausages with red cabbage and onion jam

1 cup (150g) currants
30g unsalted butter
1 tbs olive oil
4 (about 400g) red onions,
  thinly sliced
½ small red cabbage,
  very thinly sliced
1 garlic clove, chopped
½ tsp ground cinnamon
½ tsp freshly grated nutmeg
⅓ cup (75g) brown sugar
½ cup (125ml) good-quality
  balsamic vinegar
8 good-quality pork
  or beef sausages

Soak the currants in boiling water for 15 minutes, then drain.

Melt the butter with the oil in a large saucepan over medium-low heat. Add the onion and 1 teaspoon salt and cook, stirring, for 20-25 minutes until soft and lightly caramelised. Add the cabbage, garlic and spices and cook, stirring occasionally for 20-25 minutes until very tender. Add the sugar, balsamic vinegar and drained currants and cook for a further 10 minutes or until thick and syrupy.

Meanwhile, preheat a chargrill pan or barbecue to medium heat.

Cook the sausages, turning, until evenly browned and cooked through. Serve with the red cabbage and onion jam. **Serves 4**

Mexican chicken with smoky tomato salsa

¼ cup finely chopped
  flat-leaf parsley, plus
  2 cup whole flat-leaf
  parsley leaves
1 tbs ground cumin
½ cup (125ml) extra virgin
  olive oil
100ml lemon juice
4 chicken breast fillets with
  skin (wingbone attached
  – optional)*
2 vine-ripened tomatoes,
  seeds removed,
  thinly sliced
1 red onion, sliced into
  thin wedges
½ cup (40g) shaved
  parmesan

Smoky tomato salsa
3 red capsicums, quartered
5 vine-ripened tomatoes,
  halved, seeds removed
1 long red chilli, halved,
  seeds removed
1 garlic clove, chopped
1½ tbs red wine vinegar
¼ cup (60ml) extra
  virgin olive oil

Combine chopped parsley, cumin, half the oil and ¼ cup (60ml) lemon juice in a bowl. Season, then coat the chicken in the marinade. Cover and refrigerate for 30 minutes.

Meanwhile, for the smoky tomato salsa, place the capsicum, tomato and chilli, skin-side up, under a hot grill and cook for 5-6 minutes until the skins blacken. Place the capsicum and chilli in a plastic bag and seal, then set aside with the tomato to cool. When cool enough to handle, remove and discard the skin from the capsicum, chilli and tomato, then place the flesh in a food processor with the garlic, vinegar and oil. Season and blend until smooth. Transfer to a small saucepan and cook over medium heat for 10-12 minutes until thickened and reduced. Set aside.

Preheat a chargrill pan or barbecue to medium-high heat.

Cook the chicken for 3-4 minutes on each side until cooked through and golden brown. Keep warm.

Place the sliced tomato, red onion and whole parsley leaves in a bowl. Combine the remaining ¼ cup (60ml) oil and 2 tablespoons lemon juice in a bowl and season. Drizzle the dressing over the tomato and parsley salad and toss well to combine.

Spoon the tomato salsa onto serving plates with the salad. Place the chicken on top and garnish with parmesan, to serve. **Serves 4**

* Chicken breasts with wingbones attached are available from poultry shops and butchers.

Tuna wasabi burgers

500g skinless tuna fillet,
  pin-boned, chopped

2 spring onions,
  finely chopped

1 tbs sesame seeds

2 tbs fresh breadcrumbs

2 tbs soy sauce

2 garlic cloves,
  finely chopped

2 tsp finely grated ginger

½ cup coriander leaves

1 small red chilli, seeds
  removed, finely chopped

2 tsp cornflour

1½ tsp wasabi paste

1 tbs olive oil

½ cup (150g) whole-egg
  mayonnaise

4 burger buns, split, toasted

Pickled vegetables

1 small red chilli, seeds
  removed, finely chopped

1 tbs mirin

1 tbs light soy sauce

2 tsp caster sugar

2 tsp rice wine vinegar

½ telegraph cucumber

2 small carrots

Place the tuna, spring onion, sesame seeds, breadcrumbs, soy sauce, garlic, ginger, coriander, chilli, cornflour and ½ teaspoon wasabi in a food processor and pulse a few times until just combined, being careful not to over-process. Divide the mixture into 4 portions, then use damp hands to form into burgers. Cover and refrigerate for 30 minutes.

Meanwhile, for the pickled vegetables, combine the chilli, mirin, soy sauce, sugar and rice wine vinegar in a bowl, stirring to dissolve the sugar. Using a vegetable peeler, cut the cucumber and carrot into long thin ribbons. Toss with the dressing and stand for 10 minutes.

Preheat a chargrill pan or barbecue to medium-high heat.

Brush the chargrill pan or barbecue hotplate with the oil. Cook the burgers for 5 minutes each side or until the outside is charred, but the centre is still pink.

Combine the mayonnaise with the remaining 1 teaspoon wasabi, season and set aside.

Serve the burgers and toasted buns with the mayonnaise and pickled vegetables. **Serves 4**

Pina colada skewers with lime syrup

⅓ cup (90g) palm sugar *, chopped

⅓ cup (80ml) dark rum

1 small pineapple, cored, chopped into 3cm chunks

1 mango, chopped into 3cm chunks

1 papaya, chopped into 3cm chunks

Finely grated zest and juice of 4 limes

1 cup (220g) caster sugar

Mint leaves and coconut cream, to serve

Combine the palm sugar and rum in a bowl, stirring to dissolve the sugar. Toss the pineapple, mango and papaya in the sweetened rum. Cover and set aside for 1 hour.

Meanwhile, soak 12 wooden skewers in cold water for 30 minutes.

Place lime zest and juice, caster sugar and ⅓ cup (80ml) water in a saucepan over low heat, stirring to dissolve the sugar. Increase heat to medium-low and simmer for 5-6 minutes until thickened and syrupy. Set aside to cool.

Preheat chargrill pan or barbecue to medium-high heat.

Thread the fruit onto the skewers and cook for 2-3 minutes each side until caramelised and warmed through. Transfer to a serving platter, scatter with the fresh mint leaves and serve drizzled with the lime syrup and coconut cream. **Makes 12**

* Palm sugar is available from Asian food shops.

Cool yule

I adore Christmas, but not all the work. This is a simpler approach to festive fare, and what better way to celebrate the season than to cook up a feast for the people you love?

Smoked salmon vichyssoise with fir-tree croutons

30g unsalted butter

2 leeks, pale part only,
    chopped

1 onion, chopped

1 celery stalk, chopped

1 large potato,
    peeled, chopped

1L (4 cups) chicken stock
    (see 'Basics', p 296)

150g smoked salmon,
    chopped

300ml pure (thin) cream

Dill sprigs, paprika and
    extra virgin olive oil,
    to serve

Fir-tree croutons

8 white or brown
    bread slices

Sunflower oil, to shallow-fry

½ cup chopped dill

Melt the butter in a large saucepan over medium-low heat. Add the leek, onion and celery, then cook, stirring, for 2-3 minutes until softened but not coloured. Add the potato and stock, then bring to the boil over medium-high heat. Reduce heat to medium-low and simmer for 12-15 minutes until the potato is tender. Cool the soup, then stir through the chopped salmon.

In batches, blend the soup until smooth. Stir through the cream, then season to taste. Chill the vichyssoise until ready to serve.

For the fir-tree croutons, use a small Christmas tree pastry cutter to cut 2 trees from each slice of bread. Fill a frypan with 2cm sunflower oil and place over medium-high heat. In batches, fry the croutons for 1 minute each side or until crispy and golden. Remove with a slotted spoon and drain on paper towel. While still hot, dip one side of each crouton in chopped dill to coat.

Divide vichyssoise among serving bowls and garnish with dill sprigs, paprika, some freshly ground pepper and a drizzle of extra virgin olive oil. Serve with the fir-tree croutons. **Serves 6-8**

Parsnip blinis with goat's cheese

5 small (about 600g)
  parsnips
Sunflower oil, to shallow-fry
60g self-raising flour, sifted
3 eggs, plus 2 extra
  eggwhites
40g unsalted butter, melted
200g soft goat's cheese
Seeds of 1 pomegranate
Honey and micro salad
  leaves*, to serve

Slice 1 parsnip into very thin rounds (a mandoline is ideal). Heat 2cm oil in a frypan over medium-high heat. Fry parsnip rounds for 1 minute or until crisp and golden brown. Remove with a slotted spoon, drain on paper towel and set aside.

Roughly chop remaining 4 parsnips and place in a pan of cold, salted water over high heat. Bring to the boil, then reduce heat to medium-low and simmer for 12-15 minutes until tender. Drain well, then pass through a potato ricer or mash well. Season and cool slightly.

Combine the flour and whole eggs with the parsnip mash. Whisk the extra 2 eggwhites in an electric mixer until stiff peaks form, then stir half the eggwhite into the parsnip mixture to loosen. Carefully fold in the remaining eggwhites until just combined.

Brush a non-stick frypan with a little melted butter and place over medium heat. Working in batches and brushing the pan with more butter as needed, drop tablespoons of the parsnip mixture in the frypan and cook for 1-2 minutes until small bubbles appear on the surface. Turn and cook for a further 1 minute until golden and cooked through. Cool.

Arrange the blinis on a serving plate and spread each with some soft goat's cheese. Garnish with a parsnip crisp and pomegranate seeds. Just before serving, drizzle with honey and garnish with micro salad leaves. **Makes about 25**

* Micro salad leaves are available from farmers' markets and selected greengrocers.

Prawn, cannellini bean & macadamia salad

½ cup (125ml) extra virgin
    olive oil

½ cup (125ml) lemon juice

1kg cooked prawns, peeled
    (tails intact), deveined

2 x 400g cans cannellini
    beans, rinsed, drained

½ cup (75g) toasted
    macadamias, roughly
    chopped

1 preserved lemon quarter,
    white pith removed, rind
    finely chopped

250g punnet grape tomatoes

½ bunch watercress sprigs

1 tsp Dijon mustard

1 garlic clove, crushed

2 tbs finely chopped mint
    leaves, plus whole leaves
    to serve

Combine half the oil and half the lemon juice in a bowl and season. Add the prawns and toss to combine, then cover and chill for 20 minutes.

Combine cannellini beans, macadamias, preserved lemon rind, tomatoes and watercress in a bowl. Combine remaining ¼ cup (60ml) oil and ¼ cup (60ml) lemon juice in a separate bowl with the mustard, garlic and chopped mint, season, then pour over the bean mixture and toss to combine.

Transfer bean salad to a serving platter. Drain the prawns, discarding the marinade, and arrange prawns on top of the salad. Serve with extra whole mint leaves. **Serves 6**

The new roast chicken

Christmas doesn't mean spending hours in a hot kitchen waiting for the turkey to roast. This flavoursome alternative is just as impressive – yet easy on the cook!

3 garlic cloves

1 tbs chopped thyme leaves

1/3 cup (80ml) olive oil

4 x 170g skinless chicken
   breast fillets

12 slices flat pancetta*

4 slices sourdough
   bread, torn

Finely grated zest of 1 lemon

1/3 cup flat-leaf parsley

40g unsalted butter

1 tbs plain flour

1 cup (250ml) white wine

2 cups (500ml) chicken
   consomme

2 tbs dry sherry (optional)

Steamed green beans,
   to serve

Crush 1 garlic clove and place in a bowl with the thyme leaves and 2 tablespoons olive oil. Season the chicken breasts and coat in garlic oil. Wrap each chicken breast with 3 pancetta slices, slightly overlapping. Secure with kitchen string, then enclose the chicken tightly in plastic wrap and chill for 2-3 hours.

Meanwhile, preheat the oven to 190°C.

Toss the bread in 1 tablespoon olive oil. Place on a baking tray in a single layer and cook for 10 minutes or until golden and crispy. Cool, then place in a food processor with lemon zest, parsley and remaining 2 garlic cloves. Pulse until coarse crumbs and season. Set aside.

Heat the remaining 1 tablespoon olive oil in an ovenproof frypan over medium-high heat. Remove the chicken from the plastic wrap and cook, turning, for 2-3 minutes until browned all over, then roast for 10-12 minutes until the chicken is cooked through. Remove from the oven, add the butter to the frypan and baste the chicken with melted butter. Remove the chicken from the pan and rest, loosely covered with foil, while you make the gravy.

Return the frypan to medium heat and cook the flour, stirring, for 1 minute or until lightly browned. Whisk in the wine and cook for a further 2-3 minutes, then add the consomme. Bring to a simmer and cook for 5 minutes until the gravy is thickened, then add sherry.

Slice the chicken, scatter over the breadcrumbs and serve with the gravy and green beans. **Serves 4**

* Flat pancetta is available from delis.

Venison with mulled wine sauce

300ml red wine

1 tbs balsamic vinegar

3 garlic cloves, crushed

2 tsp brown sugar

1 cinnamon quill

Pinch of allspice

4 x 120g venison loins*, trimmed

1 tbs olive oil

150ml demi-glaze* or beef consomme

1 tbs cornflour

1 cup (150g) fresh or frozen redcurrants

1½ cups (180g) frozen peas

2 baby cos lettuce, outer leaves discarded

Combine red wine, balsamic, garlic, sugar, cinnamon, allspice and some salt and pepper in a bowl. Coat the venison in the marinade. Cover and marinate for at least 3 hours or overnight in the fridge, turning once or twice.

Preheat the oven to 200°C.

Remove the venison from the marinade and pat dry with paper towel. Reserve the marinade and set aside. Place the oil in a large ovenproof frypan over high heat. Add the venison and cook for 1 minute each side until browned. Transfer to the oven and roast for 6 minutes, turning once, for medium-rare. Remove from the oven, loosely cover with foil, then set aside to rest for 10 minutes.

Meanwhile, place the reserved marinade in a saucepan over medium heat and cook for 4-5 minutes until reduced by half. Add the demi-glaze and simmer for 2-3 minutes. Combine the cornflour with 2 tablespoons cold water, stirring until smooth. Stir cornflour mixture through the sauce and simmer for 1-2 minutes until thickened. Season, then strain through a fine sieve into a clean saucepan. Add the redcurrants to the pan and gently warm through. Keep warm until ready to serve.

Cook the peas in boiling, salted water until tender. Drain and refresh.

Place a few lettuce leaves on each plate and scatter with the peas. Slice the venison, arrange on plates and drizzle with a little sauce. **Serves 4**

* Order venison loins from your butcher. Demi-glaze is available from gourmet food shops and selected butchers.

Ring in the changes with recipes that are *deliciously different* from the traditional.

Pork with kumara bake and cider gravy

1.5kg French-trimmed
  pork rack
Juice of ½ lemon
2 tbs extra virgin olive oil
1 tbs thyme leaves
25g unsalted butter
1 tbs plain flour
1 tbs Dijon mustard
1 cup (250ml) cider
1½ cups (375ml) chicken
  consomme
250g jar good-quality
  apple sauce
2 tbs horseradish sauce

Kumara bake
300ml pure (thin) cream
2 tsp caraway seeds
1 garlic clove, finely chopped
¼ tsp freshly grated nutmeg
3 large (about 1.5kg),
  kumara, peeled, very
  thinly sliced (a mandoline
  is ideal)
250g havarti cheese*, grated

Preheat the oven to 230°C.

Lightly score the pork rind in a crisscross pattern, then rub with the lemon juice, oil, thyme and plenty of sea salt and black pepper. Place in a roasting pan, rind-side up, and roast for 20-25 minutes. Reduce the heat to 180°C and continue to roast for a further 1-1¼ hours until the juices run clear. Rest, loosely covered with foil, for 15 minutes.

Meanwhile, for the kumara bake, combine the cream, caraway seeds, garlic and nutmeg in a saucepan over medium heat. Bring to just below boiling point, then remove from heat and stand for 15 minutes to infuse. Grease a 1.5L baking dish and arrange one-fifth of the kumara slices in a single layer in the dish. Season, then top with one-fifth of the cheese. Pour over one-quarter of the cream mixture, then repeat the layers until all ingredients are used, finishing with a layer of cheese. Cover with a sheet of baking paper and a sheet of foil, then place in the oven on the tray below the pork. Bake the kumara for 1 hour or until tender. Remove paper and foil from the kumara bake and place dish on the top shelf. Bake, uncovered, for a further 20 minutes until bubbling and golden.

Transfer pork to a serving platter. Drain excess fat from the roasting pan, then place the pan over low heat. Melt the butter in the pan, then add the flour and cook, stirring, for 1-2 minutes until pale golden. Increase heat to medium and add mustard, cider and consomme. Bring to the boil, whisking to remove any lumps. Reduce heat to low and cook for a further 2-3 minutes until thickened. Season, then strain through a fine sieve into a warm serving jug.

Combine the apple sauce and horseradish sauce in a bowl and season. Serve the pork with the kumara bake, cider gravy and apple and horseradish sauce. **Serves 6-8**

* Havarti cheese is from delis and supermarkets; substitute gouda.

Christmas pudding surprise parcels

500ml good-quality
    vanilla bean ice cream
450g store-bought
    Christmas pudding
12 sheets fresh filo pastry*
50g unsalted butter, melted
Icing sugar, to dust

Brandy sauce
200ml pure (thin) cream
600ml milk
25g cornflour
50g caster sugar
50g unsalted butter
⅓ cup (80ml) brandy

For the brandy sauce, place the cream and milk in a saucepan over medium heat. Mix the cornflour with 2 tablespoons cold water, then add to the pan and cook for 2-3 minutes, stirring, until thickened. Remove from heat and add the sugar and butter, stirring until sugar is dissolved. Stir through the brandy and strain into a jug. Keep chilled until ready to serve.

Place 6 scoops of ice cream on a baking paper-lined baking tray, then freeze until completely firm.

Cut the pudding into 6 slices. Place each slice between 2 sheets of plastic wrap and carefully flatten with a rolling pin until 1cm thick. Remove the top sheet of plastic wrap and place a scoop of ice cream in the centre of the pudding slice. Using the bottom sheet of plastic wrap, gather the pudding around the ice cream to totally enclose. Return to the freezer for 15 minutes.

Preheat the oven to 220°C.

Working quickly, brush 1 filo sheet with some melted butter, then place another sheet on top and brush with butter. Fold sheets in half widthways. (Keep the remaining pastry sheets covered with a clean, slightly damp tea towel to prevent them from drying out.) Remove plastic wrap from a pudding ball and place in the centre of the folded filo sheets, then gather the pastry around the ball to enclose in a parcel. Return to the freezer while you repeat with remaining pudding balls and pastry.

Bake for 8 minutes or until the pastry is golden, dust with icing sugar and serve immediately with the brandy sauce. **Makes 6**

✳ Fresh filo pastry is available from the chilled section in supermarkets.

Italian spice cake

This is a very different alternative to Christmas cake. Crumbly and full of spice, its origins are in the classic Italian torta Sbrisolona from Lombardy. It's great to have with coffee or dress it up as a dessert with some mascarpone and berries.

1⅔ cups (250g) plain flour, sifted

200g fine polenta

140g blanched almonds, toasted, chopped

2 tbs cocoa, sifted, plus extra to dust

200g caster sugar

125g chilled unsalted butter, finely chopped

½ cup (125ml) sunflower oil

3 eggs, lightly beaten

1 tbs vanilla extract

1½ tsp ground cinnamon

½ tsp freshly grated nutmeg

½ tsp ground cardamom

1¼ cups (200g) whole almonds

Preheat the oven to 180°C. Grease a 24cm loose-bottomed tart pan.

Place the flour, polenta, blanched almonds, cocoa and sugar in a food processor and pulse to combine. Add the butter and pulse a few more times until just combined. Transfer the mixture to a bowl and stir in the oil, eggs, vanilla and spices until combined. Spread into the prepared pan and lightly press the whole almonds into the filling in a circular pattern.

Bake for 25 minutes or until a skewer inserted in the centre of the cake comes out clean. Remove from the oven and cool the cake in the pan for 10 minutes, then transfer to a wire rack to cool completely. Dust with cocoa powder and serve. **Serves 6-8**

Marzipan ice cream with boozy fruits

600ml pure (thin) cream
2½ cups (350ml) milk
170g marzipan*, chopped
4 egg yolks
⅓ cup (75g) caster sugar
1 tsp almond extract*

Boozy fruits
½ firmly packed cup (125g)
   dark brown sugar
100ml orange juice
1 tsp mixed spice
½ tsp cinnamon
½ tsp ground ginger
Pinch of freshly
   grated nutmeg
50g sultanas
50g currants
50g cranberries
50g candied peel
1 tbs finely grated
   orange zest
50ml dark rum

Place the cream and milk in a saucepan over medium heat and bring to just below boiling point. Remove from the heat and cool slightly.

Place the marzipan in a food processor with ½ cup (125ml) of the warm cream mixture. Whiz to a smooth paste, then return to the pan with the remaining cream mixture and bring to just below boiling point. Remove from heat and set aside.

Beat the egg yolks and sugar together in a bowl until thick and pale. Pour the warm cream mixture and almond extract into the egg yolk mixture, stirring to combine, then return the mixture to a clean saucepan. Cook over very low heat for 5-6 minutes, stirring constantly, until the mixture is thick enough to coat the back of a spoon. Transfer to a bowl, cool, then chill completely in the fridge.

Once cool, transfer the custard to an ice cream machine and churn according to manufacturer's instructions. Transfer to a plastic container and freeze until firm.

Meanwhile, for the boozy fruits, combine the sugar, orange juice and spices in a saucepan over medium-low heat and cook, stirring, until the sugar has dissolved. Bring to a simmer, then add the sultanas, currants, cranberries, peel and orange zest and cook for 5-10 minutes until syrupy. Stir through the rum, then remove from heat and cool.

Serve the boozy fruits with the marzipan ice cream. **Serves 4-8**

* Marzipan is available from supermarkets, delis and cake decorating shops. Almond extract is available from delis and gourmet food shops.

Chocolate Christmas pudding with white chocolate sauce

4 cups (760g) mixed
   dried fruit
½ cup (125ml) dark rum
250g unsalted butter,
   softened
2 firmly packed cups (500g)
   dark brown sugar
2 tsp vanilla extract
4 eggs
1 apple, coarsely grated
150g good-quality dark
   chocolate chips
1 cup (150g) plain flour,
   sifted
1 tsp mixed spice
4 cups (280g) day-old
   breadcrumbs
Finely grated zest of
   1 orange and 1 lemon
½ cup (180g) treacle

White chocolate sauce
200g white chocolate,
   chopped
300ml thickened cream
2 tbs brandy
2 tsp cornflour

Begin this recipe a day ahead.

Combine dried fruit and rum in a bowl, cover with plastic wrap and stand at room temperature to soak overnight.

The next day, grease a 2L pudding basin and place a small round of baking paper in the base. Place butter and sugar in an electric mixer and beat until thick and pale. Add vanilla, then add the eggs, one at a time, beating well after each addition. Stir in the apple and chocolate chips until combined, then stir in the flour, mixed spice, breadcrumbs, citrus zests, treacle, soaked fruit and any leftover soaking rum. Pour into the pudding basin.

Cut a square of baking paper and a square of foil. Place the paper on the foil and fold to make a pleat in the centre. Place over the basin, foil-side up, then tie with kitchen string to secure.

Place the pudding basin in a large saucepan and pour in enough boiling water to come halfway up the side of the basin. Cover with a lid and simmer over low heat for 6 hours, topping up with water as necessary. Remove the pudding basin from the saucepan and stand for 15 minutes before inverting onto a serving plate.

Meanwhile, for the white chocolate sauce, place the chocolate, cream and brandy in a saucepan over low heat and cook, stirring, for 2-3 minutes, until the chocolate has melted. Remove 1 tablespoon chocolate mixture and combine with cornflour, then stir into remaining chocolate mixture and cook, stirring, for 2-3 minutes until thickened.

Serve the pudding with the warm white chocolate sauce. The pudding will keep refrigerated for up to 1 month. To reheat the pudding, bring to room temperature, then place in a saucepan and repeat simmering process for 1 hour. **Serves 8-10**

Basics

Aioli

1 cup (250ml) sunflower oil
50ml lemon-infused extra virgin olive oil*
4 garlic cloves
2 tbs lemon juice
3 egg yolks

Combine the oils in a jug. Place garlic, lemon juice
and yolks in a food processor with a pinch of salt,
then whiz until combined. With the motor running,
add the oils in a slow, steady stream until you have
a thick mayonnaise. Season. Aioli will keep in the
fridge, covered, for up to 4 days. **Makes 1⅓ cups**
* From gourmet food shops and supermarkets.
Substitute extra virgin olive oil.

Vinaigrette

1 garlic clove
2 tbs white wine vinegar
1 tsp Dijon mustard
½ cup (125ml) extra virgin olive oil

Place garlic and 1 teaspoon salt in a mortar and
pestle and pound until a coarse paste. Stir in the
vinegar, mustard and some freshly ground black
pepper, then gradually add the oil in a steady
stream, whisking constantly, until you have
a thick emulsion. **Makes about ⅔ cup**

Chicken stock

1.5kg whole chicken
1 onion, chopped
1 carrot, chopped
1 leek, trimmed, chopped
1 bay leaf
2-3 thyme sprigs
2 flat-leaf parsley stalks
6-8 whole black peppercorns

Begin this recipe a day ahead.

Wash the chicken inside and out, then place
in a large stockpot with 3.5L cold water. Add the
onion, carrot, leek, bay leaf, thyme sprigs, parsley
stalks and peppercorns. Bring to the boil over
medium heat, then reduce heat to very low and
simmer uncovered, skimming foam and impurities
from the surface occasionally, for 1½ hours.
(Don't let the stock simmer too rapidly, or it
will be cloudy.)

Allow the stock to cool slightly, then strain
through a muslin-lined sieve. Discard the
vegetables and herbs, and reserve the chicken
meat for use in sandwiches and pies.

Cool the stock completely, then place in the
refrigerator to chill overnight.

The next day, use a large spoon to scrape off the
fat from the surface and discard. The stock will
keep in airtight containers in the fridge for up to
3 days or frozen for up to 3 months. **Makes 3L**

Pesto

2 firmly packed cups basil leaves
⅓ cup (50g) pine nuts
2 garlic cloves
1¼ cups (100g) grated parmesan
150ml extra virgin olive oil

Place the basil, nuts, garlic and parmesan in a food processor and whiz until combined. With the motor running, add the oil in a slow, steady stream until a smooth paste. Pesto will keep in the fridge, under a thin layer of oil, for up to 1 week. **Makes 2½ cups**

Chocolate ganache

450g good-quality dark chocolate, chopped
175g unsalted butter
600ml thickened cream
¼ cup (90g) liquid glucose*

Place chocolate and butter in a bowl set over a pan of simmering water (don't let the bowl touch the water), stirring until smooth. Remove from heat.

Place the cream and glucose in a pan, bring to just below boiling point. Pour over the chocolate mixture and stir until smooth. Chill for 30 minutes or until thick. The ganache will keep chilled for up to 1 week – gently reheat before use. **Makes 4 cups**
* Liquid glucose is available from supermarkets.

Proper custard

5 egg yolks
¼ cup (55g) caster sugar
2 cups (500ml) pure (thin) cream
1 vanilla bean, split, seeds scraped

Gently whisk the egg yolks and sugar together in a bowl. Place the cream and vanilla pod and seeds in a saucepan over medium heat and bring to just below boiling point. Pour the cream mixture into the egg mixture, whisking to combine.

Return the custard mixture to a clean pan and place over low heat. Cook for 5-6 minutes, stirring constantly, until the mixture is thick enough to coat the back of the spoon – watch carefully as you don't want to scramble the eggs.

Strain into a jug, then cover the surface closely with plastic wrap to prevent a skin forming. Serve warm or chilled. **Makes 2¹/₂ cups**

Sugar syrup

1 cup (220g) caster sugar

Place sugar in a pan with 1 cup (250ml) water over medium-low heat, stirring until the sugar has dissolved. Increase heat to medium and simmer for 5 minutes until slightly reduced. Cool, then keep in the fridge for up to 1 month. **Makes 1½ cups**

Index

Aioli 296
Angel hair pasta with larb ... 142
Apple & goat's cheese salad.. 10
Apple tarte Tatin.................. 30
Bacon & egg fried rice 138
Baked custards 222
Barbecue tapas.................. 252
beef
   Beef carpaccio with beetroot
     and sauce gribiche 84
   Beef on lemongrass skewers
     with cucumber salad.... 258
   Chateaubriand with
     bearnaise and
     drunken potatoes 214
   Chilli for a crowd 230
   Chinese braised beef 234
   Fillet of beef with
     three-mustard sauce.... 34
   Onglet with Cafe
     de Paris butter.............. 22
Beetroot & goat's
   cheese jalousie................ 94
berries
   Blueberry, mango
     & praline trifle 156
   Caramel raspberry tarts
     with orange cream 50

Chocolate-swirl meringues
   with strawberries 154
Rhubarb & strawberry
   crumbles...................... 54
Strawberry soup with
   goat's milk sorbet....... 122
Black-bottom lemon meringue
   ice cream pie 160
Black Forest Eton mess....... 52
Blueberry, mango
   & praline trifle.............. 156
Bouillabaisse in a bag.......... 16
cakes *see also* **desserts**
   Chocolate butterscotch
     layer cake 174
   Coconut crepe cake.......... 26
   Ginger cakes with
     chilli icing 148
   Italian spice cake............ 290
   Little black dress
     chocolate cake............ 126
   Orange lavender
     syrup cake 24
   Passion cake 218
   Ricotta & Marsala
     cheesecake................. 198
   Turkish delight
     cheesecake................. 168
   Yoghurt cake with
     sangria-poached fruit ...102
Caramel raspberry tarts
   with orange cream 50
Cauliflower cheese soup ... 228
Champagne & asparagus
   risotto with oysters 204
Chateaubriand with bearnaise
   and drunken potatoes 214

cheese
Apple & goat's
   cheese salad................. 10
Beetroot & goat's
   cheese jalousie............. 94
Cheese & fig tarts 180
Haloumi with
   Mediterranean salad .. 250
Melon, pecorino
   & prosciutto salad 184
Parsnip blinis
   with goat's cheese 276
Ricotta & Marsala
   cheesecake 198
Twice-baked soufflé 12
Warm barley & mushroom
   salad with Taleggio 226
Yesterday's croissants...... 14
cheesecakes *see* **cakes**
Chermoula fish
   with tahini sauce 256
chicken
Angel hair pasta
   with larb..................... 142
Barbecue tapas 252
Chicken stock 296
Chicken, tomato
   & spinach curry 36
Grown-up chicken
   nuggets......................... 64
Jerk chicken 96
Mexican chicken with smoky
   tomato salsa 266
Panko-crumbed chicken
   caesar salad 146
Smoky Spanish chicken ... 112
The new roast chicken ... 280

chilled desserts *see also*
cakes; desserts; tarts

Baked custards 222

Black-bottom
    lemon meringue
    ice cream pie 160

Blueberry, mango
    & praline trifle 156

Chocolate-chip tiramisu ...196

Ice cream terrine............ 172

Marzipan ice cream
    with boozy fruits 292

Peach Melba buttermilk
    puddings 74

Pimm's jellies................. 100

Pineapple caramels 150

Strawberry soup with
    goat's milk sorbet....... 122

Watermelon mojito
    ice blocks 78

Chilli for a crowd............... 230

Chinese braised beef 234

Chinese pork buns 134

chocolate

Black Forest Eton mess ... 52

Chocolate & rum bread
    & butter pudding 246

Chocolate butterscotch
    layer cake 174

Chocolate-chip tiramisu .. 196

Chocolate Christmas pudding
    with white-choc sauce.. 294

Chocolate ganache......... 297

Chocolate mousse tarts... 162

Chocolate-swirl meringues
    with strawberries 154

Chocolatini 220

Jam & chocolate roly poly
    with proper custard 244

Little black dress
    chocolate cake............ 126

Millionaire's eclairs........ 158

Self-saucing chocolate
    pudding 242

Triple-chocolate cookies.. 170

Chocolatini with
    chocolate 'body paint' 220

Christmas pudding
    surprise parcels 288

Coconut crepe cake 26

Corn soup with avocado, lime
    and grilled prawns 108

Crab, coconut & green
    mango salad.................... 62

Crisp pork belly with
    sour peach salad.............. 72

Custard.............................. 297

desserts *see also* **cakes;**
chilled desserts; tarts

Black Forest Eton mess ... 52

Chocolate & rum bread
    & butter pudding 246

Chocolate Christmas pudding
    with white-choc sauce ..294

Chocolate-swirl meringues
    with strawberries 154

Christmas pudding
    surprise parcels 288

Jam & chocolate roly poly
    with proper custard 244

Lemon & lime curd with
    ricotta and blueberries ...98

Mille-feuille with praline
    cream and raspberries ...28

Pina colada skewers
    with lime syrup 270

Poached pears with
    chocolate mousse....... 124

Rhubarb & strawberry
    crumbles...................... 54

Self-saucing chocolate
    pudding 242

Double dip 202

Dirty rice with salmon.......... 38

drinks

Chocolatini 220

Scarlatini 178

duck

Duck breast with
    spiced orange sauce..... 18

Duck cassoulet 240

Duck with cherry sauce.. 118

Duck wonton soup.......... 132

Eggplant pesto timballos... 182

Farfalle with sausage ragu .. 186

Fillet of beef with
    three-mustard sauce 34

fish

Chermoula fish with
    tahini sauce 256

Dirty rice with salmon...... 38

Fish pie 238

Hot-smoked trout & rice
    salad with mint pesto..... 86

Smoked salmon vichyssoise
    with fir-tree croutons... 274

Soba noodles with
    hot-smoked salmon ... 144

Spicy fish with Arabic orange
    & nasturtium salad 46

Spicy fishcakes with pickled-
    ginger mayonnaise 130

Tuna wasabi burgers...... 268

Tuna with green
    tea noodles 42

Vodka-cured ocean trout
    with soy jelly 110

fruit *see also* **berries**

Apple tarte Tatin 30

Crisp pork belly with
sour peach salad 72

Lemon & lime curd 98

Mango risotto with
tropical fruit 76

Orange lavender
syrup cake 24

Passion cake 218

Peach Melba buttermilk
puddings 74

Pina colada skewers 270

Pineapple caramels 150

Poached pears with
chocolate mousse 124

Watermelon mojito
ice blocks 78

Yoghurt cake with
sangria-poached fruit ...102

Garlic prawn pâté 82

Gin & tonic tart 166

Ginger cakes with
chilli icing 148

Grown-up chicken nuggets .. 64

Haloumi with
Mediterranean salad 250

Heirloom tomato
pastry hearts 210

Herb-rubbed lamb cutlets ... 40

Hot-smoked trout & rice salad
with mint pesto 86

ice cream *see* **chilled desserts**

Ice cream terrine 172

It's a lamb wrap 70

Italian spice cake 290

Jam & chocolate roly poly
with proper custard 244

Jerk chicken 96

lamb

Herb-rubbed lamb cutlets ..40

It's a lamb wrap 70

Lamb burgers with
harissa mayonnaise ... 262

Lamb en croute 206

Lamb tian 120

Massaman curry lamb
shanks 232

Lemon & lime curd with fresh
ricotta and blueberries 98

Little black dress
chocolate cake 126

Lobster spaghetti 208

Lobster Thermidor 114

Mango risotto with
tropical fruit 76

Marzipan ice cream
with boozy fruits 292

Massaman curry
lamb shanks 232

Melon, pecorino
& prosciutto salad 184

Mexican chicken with
smoky tomato salsa 266

Mille-feuille with praline
cream and raspberries 28

Millionaire's eclairs 158

Onglet with
Cafe de Paris butter 22

Orange lavender syrup cake ...24

Panko-crumbed chicken
caesar salad 146

Parsnip blinis with
goat's cheese 276

Passion cake 218

pasta and noodles

Angel hair pasta
with larb 142

Farfalle with
sausage ragu 186

Lobster spaghetti 208

Pasta genovese 194

Soba noodles with
hot-smoked salmon ... 144

Spaghetti with mussels ...190

Tuna with
green tea noodles 42

Peach Melba buttermilk
puddings 74

Pesto 297

Pimm's jellies 100

Pina colada skewers 270

Pineapple caramels 150

Poached pears with
chocolate mousse 124

pork

Chinese pork buns 134

Crisp pork belly with
sour peach salad 72

Pork chops with wild
mushroom sauce 48

Pork with kumara bake ... 286

Prawn & taramasalata
rice paper rolls 58

Prawn, cannellini bean
& macadamia salad 278

Prawns with tomato
ice cream 66

quail

Quail with rose petals
and yoghurt 216

Salt & pepper quail 136

Rhubarb & strawberry
crumbles 54

Ricotta & Marsala
cheesecake 198

Roasted tomato soup 88

salads

Apple & goat's cheese
salad 10

Crab, coconut & green
mango salad 62

Haloumi with
Mediterranean salad... 250

Hot-smoked trout & rice
salad with mint pesto 86

Melon, pecorino
& prosciutto salad 184

Panko-crumbed
chicken caesar salad.... 146

Prawn, cannellini bean
& macadamia salad.... 278

Warm barley & mushroom
salad with Taleggio 226

Salt & pepper quail
with chilli sauce.............. 136

sauces, dips and condiments

Aioli................................. 296

Custard 297

Double dip 202

Pesto............................... 297

Sugar syrup 297

Vinaigrette 296

Sausages with red cabbage
and onion jam................. 264

Scallops with cauliflower puree
and jamon crumbs 106

Scarlatini............................ 178

seafood *see also* **fish**

Bouillabaisse in a bag 16

Champagne & asparagus
risotto with oysters 204

Corn soup with avocado, lime
and grilled prawns...... 108

Crab, coconut & green
mango salad 62

Garlic prawn pâté............. 82

Lobster spaghetti 208

Lobster Thermidor......... 114

Prawn & taramasalata
rice paper rolls 58

Prawn, cannellini bean
& macadamia salad.... 278

Prawns with tomato
ice cream 66

Scallops with
cauliflower puree 106

Spaghetti with mussels... 190

Spicy prawns with
harissa couscous........ 254

Squid with chilli lime salt... 60

Self-saucing chocolate
pudding........................... 242

Smoked salmon vichyssoise
with fir-tree croutons..... 274

Smoky Spanish chicken 112

Soba noodles with
hot-smoked salmon 144

soups

Cauliflower cheese soup.. 228

Corn soup with avocado,
lime and prawns 108

Duck wonton soup.......... 132

Roasted tomato soup 88

Smoked salmon vichyssoise
with fir-tree croutons... 274

Spaghetti with mussels 190

Spicy fish with Arabic orange
& nasturtium salad 46

Spicy fishcakes with pickled-
ginger mayonnaise......... 130

Spicy prawns with
harissa couscous............ 254

Squid with chilli lime salt 60

Still-life tart 90

Strawberry soup with
goat's milk sorbet 122

Sugar syrup........................ 297

tarts

Apple tarte Tatin 30

Caramel raspberry tarts
with orange cream 50

Cheese & fig tarts 180

Chocolate mousse tarts... 162

Gin & tonic tart 166

Heirloom tomato hearts... 210

Still-life tart...................... 90

The new roast chicken 280

tomato

Chicken, tomato
& spinach curry 36

Heirloom tomato hearts .. 210

Roasted tomato soup 88

Tomato, mascarpone
& rocket pizza 192

Triple-chocolate fudge
cookies 170

Tuna wasabi burgers.......... 268

Tuna with green tea noodles and
black vinegar dressing..... 42

Turkish delight cheesecake..168

Twice-baked soufflé............. 12

Venison with mulled
wine sauce...................... 282

Vinaigrette.......................... 296

Vodka-cured ocean trout
with soy jelly 110

Warm barley & mushroom
salad with Taleggio......... 226

Watermelon mojito
ice blocks.......................... 78

Yesterday's croissants.......... 14

Yoghurt cake with
sangria-poached fruit 102

With thanks

A COOKBOOK IS rarely the work of a single person and I've been fortunate to have a wonderful team to support me in what has been a huge project.

Firstly, my great appreciation goes to the News Magazines executive team for once more allowing me to indulge my passion and create this special book under the *delicious.* brand. Also thanks to ABC Books and HarperCollins Publishers for this opportunity and your enthusiasm and patience.

A heartfelt thank you to *delicious.* editor-in-chief Trudi Jenkins (we share our 10-year anniversary on the magazine as I write these acknowledgments), for your faith in the book and your guidance, wisdom and ongoing support particularly when the going got tough – and it did.

Thanks also to the brilliant art team, headed up by Scott Cassidy, and including the lovely Shannon Keogh, for your ideas and creative input. Thanks, too, to senior designer Steph Westcott for holding the fort on the magazine. Special thanks must go to the very talented Jacqui Porter, art director on the book. Her unique eye and dedication to detail has created something quite special. And sincere thanks also to Carla Grossetti for her work as project editor.

The editorial team on *delicious.* is such a lovely group to be part of. A million thank yous go to acting managing editor Annette Farnsworth for keeping a watchful eye on things and being the only one brave enough to make the call to our publisher when we were running late. Thanks to chief subeditor Shannon Harley for your cheery smile and hard work, and also to Stephanie Vander Linden and Alice Lindley (a budding stylist in her own right). It would be wrong of me not to make special mention of Alison Pickel, *delicious.* senior subeditor, who returned from holidays to be plunged headfirst into the final editing of the book and has done such an incredible job. I've watched Alison progress through the ranks on the magazine with pure dedication and hard work. I'm quite sure I'll be asking her for a job one day!

The beautiful images of my recipes are the work of what is, in my humble opinion, the very best team in the business. The genius of stylist David Morgan and the truly exceptional work of photographer Brett Stevens – I'm lost to find the words to describe your exceptional talents so shall just do it in one: respect.

I'm extremely fortunate to have a wonderful food team, so I send an especially big hug to Jessica Brook and Phoebe Wood who cooked alongside me each day when we were shooting.

Jessica also managed to keep all the testing going for the magazine and Phoebe did such a fantastic job collating and editing the recipes, while at the same time managing to keep me sane (well, almost).

My family is an amazing support and my love and thanks, as always, go to them.

And last, but by no means least, this book is dedicated to *delicious.* readers. Those who have been with us from the beginning and those who have just discovered us. None of this would be possible if you didn't love what we do. You are all simply the best.

THANKS TO THE FOLLOWING STOCKISTS
Aeria Country Floors stores nationally, aeria.com.au

Genevieve Lethu Woollahra (02) 9327 8307, genevievelethu.com.au

Grain de Couleur order online, graindecouleur.com

Ici et la stores nationally, icietla.com.au

Mud Australia stockists nationally (02) 9389 5580, mudaustralia.com

Papaya stockists nationally (02) 9386 9980, papaya.com.au

Spence & Lyda Surry Hills (02) 9212 6747, spenceandlyda.com.au

· ABC Books The ABC 'Wave' device is a trademark of the Australian Broadcasting Corporation and is used under licence by HarperCollins*Publishers* Australia. The *delicious.* trademark is used under licence from The Australian Broadcasting Corporation and News Magazines.

First published in Australia in November 2011 by HarperCollins*Publishers* Australia Pty Ltd ABN 36 009 913 517 harpercollins.com.au

HarperCollins*Publishers* Level 13, 201 Elizabeth Street, Sydney, NSW, 2000, Australia; 31 View Road, Glenfield, Auckland, 0627, NZ; 1A Hamilton House, Connaught Place, New Delhi, 110 001, India; 77–85 Fulham Palace Road, London, W6 8JB, UK; 2 Bloor Street East, Toronto, Ontario, M4W 1A8, Canada; 10 East 53rd Street, New York, NY, 10022, USA

National Library of Australia Cataloguing-in-Publication data:
Little, Valli
delicious. Simply the Best/Valli Little
ISBN: 9780733330261 (pbk.)
Includes index
Cooking
Australian Broadcasting Corporation
641.5

Food Director Valli Little **Photography** Brett Stevens **Styling** David Morgan
Creative Director Scott Cassidy **Project Art Director** Jacqui Porter **Art Director** Shannon Keogh
Managing Editor Annette Farnsworth **Project Editor** Carla Grossetti
Subeditors Shannon Harley, Alison Pickel **Food Preparation** Jessica Brook, Phoebe Wood
Publisher ABC Magazines Liz White **Publishing Editor ABC Magazines** Marija Beram
Managing Editor ABC Magazines Diane Parks
delicious. **Editor-in-chief** Trudi Jenkins **CEO, News Magazines** Sandra Hook

Additional photography: Ben Dearnley (p 284-285), John Dennis (p 68-69),
Jared Fowler (p 92-93), Mark Roper (p 80,92-93, 236-237), Kieran Scott (p 236-237),
Jeremy Simons (p 93), Ian Wallace (p 20-21)

Colour Reproduction by Graphic Print Group, Adelaide, SA
Printed in China by RR Donnelley (on 157gsm Matt Art)

5 4 3 2   12 13